THE READING TEACHER'S ALMANAC

Hundreds of Practical Ideas, Games, Activities, Bulletin Boards, and Reproducibles for Every Month of the Year

Patricia Tyler Muncy

Illustrated by Janice Mori Gallagher

THE CENTER FOR APPLIED RESEARCH IN EDUCATION
West Nyack, New York 10995

10 9 8 7 6 5 4 3 2 1

Library of Congress Cataloging-in-Publication Data

Muncy, Patricia Tyler
    The reading teacher's almanac : hundreds of practical ideas,
games, activities, bulletin boards, and reproducibles for every
month of the year / Patricia Tyler Muncy ; illustrated by Janice
Mori Gallagher.
        p.   cm.
    ISBN 0-87628-791-7
    1. Reading—Aids and devices—Handbooks, manuals, etc. 2. Reading
(Elementary)—Handbooks, manuals, etc. I. Center for Applied
Research in Education. II. Title.
LB1573.39.M86 1991
372.4′1—dc20   91-11305
                                                                              CIP

ISBN 0-87628-791-7

**THE CENTER FOR APPLIED
RESEARCH IN EDUCATION**
West Nyack, New York 10995

Printed in the United States of America

About the Author

Patricia Tyler Muncy is the Reading Supervisor for grades K-12 and the Elementary Supervisor for grades K-4 of Wayne County, Ohio's seven school districts. She holds an M.S. in Reading Supervision. She is also an experienced classroom reading teacher and remedial reading teacher.

Mrs. Muncy is the author of a variety of practical teaching/learning materials. These include *Word Puzzles* (Fearon-Pitman Publishers, 1974); *Froggie Alphabet Game* (Ideal School Supply Company, 1976); and seven books of duplicator masters published by Instructor Curriculum Materials—*Word Play, Books A and B* (1977), *Handwriting, Books A, B, and C* (1979), and *Dictionary Skills, Grades 1 and 2* and *Grades 5 and 6* (1980).

She is the author of *Complete Book of Illustrated K-3 Alphabet Games and Activities* (The Center, 1980), *Springboards to Creative Thinking* (The Center, 1985), and is one of the authors of the Scott, Foresman and Company spelling programs *Spelling: Words and Skills* (1984) and *Scott, Foresman Spelling* (1988).

Mrs. Muncy is also on the Editorial Advisory Board of The Center's *Primary Teacher's Ready-to-Use Activities Program,* as well as being a contributing author to that program.

ABOUT THIS ALMANAC

Developed for elementary classroom teachers and reading specialists, *The Reading Teacher's Almanac* provides hundreds of ready-to-use activities and games for teaching and reinforcing basic reading skills. The *Almanac* is organized by the months of the school year, and each monthly section includes a variety of original activities, games, worksheets, bulletin boards, flash cards, bookmarks, manipulatives, and projects. In addition, for each month you will find:

- *Instruction tip of the month,* which will give you step-by-step techniques for improving the effectiveness of reading instruction in your classroom. For example, in October you will find specific group response techniques to stamp out wandering minds during reading class. In January, you will get tips for linking reading and writing.
- *Book report activity sheets* are designed to encourage children to read for pleasure and to replace the standard oral book report format with motivational book-based activities.
- *Story extension activities* to use with any story in a basal reader or trade book.
- *Bonus idea of the month* offers you ideas for teaching new sight words, making envelopes to hold game pieces, making book covers, and more.

CONTENTS

NOVEMBER • 75

DECEMBER • 109

JANUARY • 141

FEBRUARY • 179

MARCH • 203

APRIL • 231

MAY/JUNE • 255

WORD LISTS • 287

AUGUST/ SEPTEMBER

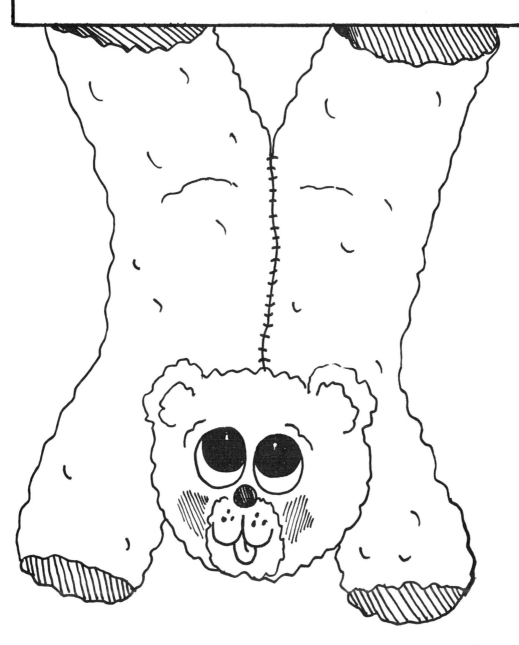

NEW YEAR'S RESOLUTIONS

We usually think of New Year's resolutions about the first of January. However, for teachers, New Year's resolutions should be formed in August before the beginning of a new school year. This is the time to think about the instructional techniques we use in our classrooms and the ways we can make our reading instruction even more effective. Remember, even the best instruction can be improved upon.

On the next page you will find an excellent classroom reading teacher's New Year's Resolutions list. You may wish to photocopy it, laminate it, and tape it on your desk or place it in some equally visible location to serve as a constant reminder. Ample space has been left at the end of the list for you to add your own additional New Year's Resolutions.

Take time now to think about your reading instruction and develop the rest of your New Year's Resolutions list.

The Classroom Reading Teacher's
New Year's Resolutions

1. I will structure my instruction to make maximum use of available learning time.

2. I will use group response techniques to maximize student involvement and student learning.

3. I will always make certain students clearly understand how to do all assigned reading seatwork activities before they work independently.

4. Whenever appropriate, I will model for the students the thinking process to be used in arriving at the correct answer.

5. I will provide the students with guided practice and make sure each one is firm in the process needed to do the assignment with a high degree of accuracy before letting them proceed independently with the assignment.

6. Except in first and second grade, I will *not* use round-robin oral reading in my reading classes.

7. I will actively promote reading for pleasure with my students.

8. I will find ways to incorporate writing into the reading program on a frequent basis.

12 HELPFUL HINTS FOR CONSTRUCTING GAMES AND TEACHING DEVICES

Use these hints throughout the year to make the construction of games and teaching devices easier and to make the activities more attractive and usable.

1. To save time and extend the use of an instructional game, prepare the gameboard omitting the words to be practiced. After the gameboard has been laminated, add the words, letters, or phonics elements to be practiced, writing them along the pathway using a transparency pen. When the students have played the game a number of times and no longer need practice on those words or skills, simply wipe off the words (etc.) with a damp cloth and write new words or phonics items along the pathway. Thus, the gameboard can be used over and over throughout the year, providing the drill needed at that particular time. In this way the gameboard can also be multipurpose, allowing flexibility in the skills the game will reinforce at a given time.

2. Words written on gameboard laminated surfaces with transparency pens have a definite tendency to smear as game markers are moved along the pathway. To overcome this problem you may want to write the words on the gameboard using a *permanent* fine line pen such as a Stanford's Sharpie pen. Later, when you are ready to put new words or phonics items on the gameboard, spray hair spray on the words and wipe them off with a soft cloth. The permanent ink is quickly and easily removed and the gameboard is ready for you to write the new words!

3. Papermate Fine-Line Flair Pens work best for writing words on game cards. The ink will not bleed through to the back side of items made with the lighter weight materials such as oaktag, coverstock, and heavy art paper.

4. Stanford Sharpie Fine-Point Pens work very well for outlining drawings on gameboards and other activities made on railroad board or posterboard. Because they are permanent ink pens, they will not smear when you color in pictures with broad-tip markers.

5. Permanent-ink broad-felt-tip markers are excellent for coloring in pictures on gameboards, etc. made on railroad board or posterboard. To get a smooth, deep color appearance, color the picture once with the permanent markers, then go back and color them in again. All of the Magic Marker streaks will disappear!

6. Watercolor felt-tip markers work best for games and activities constructed on the lighter weight cardboards such as oaktag or coverstock. The water color markers will not bleed through to the back surface.

7. Crayon can be used for coloring games and instructional devices that will be laminated only if the crayon is applied lightly. CAUTION: Heavy

application will result in melted streaks of crayon wax when the object is laminated.

8. White felt-tip markers can be purchased from school supply stores and office supply stores. White felt-tip markers are not found in the packaged sets of markers. They are packaged separately. The white markers are excellent for marking on gameboards made on dark blue, brown, or black railroad board or posterboard.

9. A good set of colored pencils is a must for constructing teacher-made instructional games and teaching devices. The colored pencil sets usually found in discount stores and drug stores do not have the soft lead that will produce smooth, rich colors on your teacher-made items. You will want to avoid these. Instead, purchase a Prismacolor Colored Pencil Set or a Venus Colored Pencil Set. These brands of colored pencils can be purchased through school supply catalogs and through office supply stores.

10. When you wish to erase lines from the posterboard or railroad board surface of a gameboard under construction, use a gum eraser to do the erasing. A gum eraser will not leave markings or remove the color from the surface of the cardboard. Most other types of erasers leave noticeable marks that detract from the final appearance of the gameboard.

11. Only use rubber cement for gluing things to gameboards before laminating. When laminated, the glue marks will be invisible. If white school glue is used, the glue dabs will show through when the object is laminated!

12. An X-acto® knife (a type of art knife) or a single-edge razor blade will work well for cutting slots in a teacher-made tachist-o-scope and for slicing open laminated manila envelopes.

EFFECTIVE INSTRUCTION TIP OF THE MONTH

GROUP PARTICIPATION TECHNIQUES: SIGNALED RESPONSES

Begin the school year implementing group participation activities in your classroom. Group participation activities will increase the reading skill development of students in your classroom by keeping their attention focused on learning more of the time. Group participation activities are effective with both small and large groups and are appropriate for primary, elementary, and junior high school classrooms.

Think of your class for a minute. When you ask a question and call on one student to respond, many of the other students in the group simply do not participate in the thought process needed to come up with the correct answer. As soon as you call on a student, the rest of the students can disengage. They simply do not need to think of the correct answer. When students are not actively thinking through the questions, developing their own answers, and listening to see if they were correct, valuable learning opportunities are being lost and children are not learning as much as they could have been learning.

Group participation activities keep *all* students in the group focused on the learning activity, thinking through *each* answer and responding to *every* question. Group participation activities require responses from all students, not just the one called on.

One category of group participation techniques is signaled response activities. Here are some excellent examples of signaled responses.

Have the students show their answers with hand signals.

1. Pronounce words with one, two, or three syllables. Have students hold up one finger if they think the word contains one syllable. Have them hold up two fingers if the word contains two syllables or three fingers if the word is a three-syllable word.
2. Ask the students a series of true or false questions about the story. Have the students make a T with their fingers if they think the statement is true. Have them form an F with their fingers if they think the statement is false.

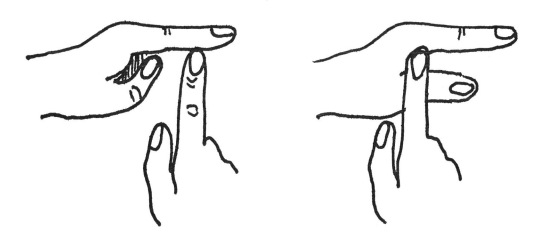

Or, instead of asking a series of true or false questions, you may wish to intersperse an occasional true or false question (to which all students signal their answers) among the discussion questions. In this way all students must pay attention to the questions and stay involved.

3. Pronounce words containing long or short vowel sounds. Have the students hold their index fingers in a straight horizontal position to represent a long vowel mark if they think the word you pronounce has a long vowel sound. Have them hold their index fingers and thumbs in a curved position to represent a short vowel mark if they think the word you say contains a short vowel.

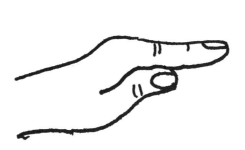

Long Vowel Signal   **Short Vowel Signal**

4. Pronounce pairs of words that are either synonyms or antonyms. If the words are synonyms, have the students form an S with their fingers. If the words are antonyms, have the students form an A with their fingers.

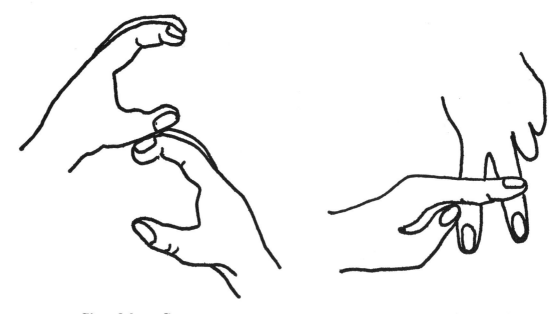

Signal for a Synonym   **Signal for an Antonym**

5. Say pairs of words, some of which are rhyming, some of which are non-rhyming. Have the students put "thumbs up" if they think the pair of words you say are rhyming words. Have them put "thumbs down" if they think the words do not rhyme.

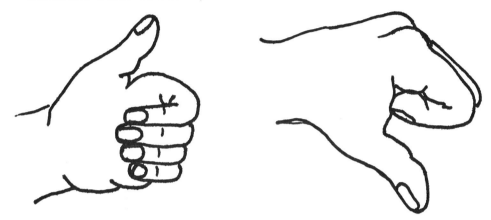

6. Have the students touch their lips with an index finger if they think the word you write on the chalkboard contains a silent letter. Have them put one of their hands behind an ear in a listening position if they think they can hear all of the vowels in the word and there are no silent vowels.

7. Have students select the correct answer to a multiple choice question and signal their answers by holding up one, two, three, or four fingers to correspond with the number of the correct answer. If the multiple choice answers are indicated by letters instead of numbers, have the students use their fingers to form the shape of the letter for the correct answer choice.

Have the students show their answers with other types of signals.

1. Give each student two yellow construction paper circles (approximately 3″ in diameter), one with a smiling face drawn on it, the other with a

frowning face. Have students hold up the smiling face circle in front of their chests if they think the answer given by another student is correct. Have them hold up the frowning face circle if they think the answer is incorrect.

2. Give each student two unlined 3″ × 5″ file cards, one with the word "yes" printed on it with a felt-tip pen, one with the word "no" printed on it. Say pairs of words. Have the students hold up the "yes" card if a pair of words contains the same vowel sound. Have them hold up the "no" card if a pair of words does not contain the same vowel sound.

3. Have students smile a big smile if they think the pair of words you say are rhyming words. Have them scowl if they think the words do not rhyme.

The possibilities of interesting, creative ways for students to signal responses are endless. Simply think of the question-answer task students will be performing, then think of a way all students can signal their individual answers to you.

The benefits of these signaled response activities are unquestionable. They maintain students' interest, they force all students to stay on task, and they force all students to participate in thinking about and answering every question. An additional strong bonus is that this type of group response allows you immediate feedback on the degree of understanding and mastery of the skill on the part of each individual student in the class. When you ask a question and see part of the class signaling one answer and part of the class signaling another answer, you will know that a large number of the students are confused and need further instruction on the skill before proceeding.

You will certainly want to add signaled response techniques to the repertoire of instructional methods you use in your reading class. These techniques are worthy of very frequent use.

> NOTE: Additional ideas of other group participation techniques are found in the October "Effective Instruction Tip of the Month."

READING SEATWORK ACTIVITIES FOR GRADES 1–2

First grade provides a special challenge to teachers to devise worthwhile reading seatwork activities for the students to do when they have finished assigned workbook pages and duplicator worksheets. Here are some good possibilities:

Letter-Sound Relationships

1. Have students cut pictures from magazines or catalogs and glue them on paper to create specified consonant sound posters.
2. Using watercolor paints or tempera paints, have children create vowel sound picture posters. Brainstorm together words containing the selected vowel sound. Print the words on the chalkboard. Let the children paint pictures of objects containing the selected vowel sound on sheets of art paper. When pictures are dry, have individual children tell you what each picture represents on his/her poster. Using a black marker, print the identifying word beneath each picture on the child's sound poster.

   > VARIATION: Have students create initial consonant or initial consonant blend picture posters.

Letter Recognition

1. Using magnetic plastic letters, have pairs of students take turns putting letters in alphabetical order.
2. Have students print letters in alphabetical order on magic slates, pull up the two plastic sheets to erase, and print them again.
3. Using a red crayon, have students underline all of the words they can find that begin with a specified letter on a page from an old catalog or children's magazine.

Sight Word Recognition

1. Let students work in pairs with flashcards, practicing sight word recognition.
2. Print newly introduced words on a transparency. Using an overhead projector, project the words on a chalkboard. Make sure students know what

each word says. Let students take turns writing the words on the chalk-board by tracing over the projected words with chalk, erasing, then tracing over the projected words again. Each time the student prints a word, he/she should softly say the word aloud.

> VARIATION: The same procedure can be used with simple sentences containing newly introduced words, or with sentences from a dictated group language experience story. In each case, make sure the students can read the sentence(s) correctly before beginning to write.

3. Using water and a water color paintbrush, let pairs of students "paint" on the chalkboard words needing sight word recognition drill. After each word is "painted" on the chalkboard, both students in the pair say the word softly aloud in unison. "Painted" words evaporate in a couple of minutes.
4. Let students write sight words in clay (or playdough). Give students a piece of waxed paper and a chunk of clay. Have them flatten the clay on the waxed paper surface, then print sight words to be practiced in the clay using their pencils. After a word has been printed, the student can smooth the surface of the clay, then print the next word. Sight words practiced in this way should be printed on the chalkboard or on paper for easy reference as the children write the words.
5. Let students print new words on magic slates, erase, and print them again. Each time the child prints a word, he/she should say it aloud softly.

Comprehension

1. Have each student draw a picture of a character in the story and then write the character's name beneath the picture.
2. Have each student draw a picture of a favorite part of the basal reader story and write a sentence about the picture (using invented spelling).
3. Have students fold a sheet of paper in half, then draw two pictures showing what happened in the basal reader story or in a library book story read aloud to the class by the teacher.
4. Have students copy a sentence from the basal reader on writing paper. Then have them draw a picture to go with the sentence.
5. Cut a number of interesting pictures from magazines. Have students select a picture, glue it on writing paper, and write a sentence about the picture (using invented spelling).

Oral Reading

1. Let students sit in pairs and quietly take turns reading the story aloud, helping each other with any unknown words.

Promoting Enjoyment of Books

1. Have students draw a picture of a favorite place to read a storybook.
2. Let students draw a picture of a favorite storybook character.
3. Encourage students to read library books/look at pictures in picture books.

READING SEATWORK ACTIVITIES FOR GRADES 3–6

The following seatwork activities can be used with stories in any basal reader or children's book.

Have students:

1. Draw a picture of the setting of the story.
2. Write a description of the setting of the story, using a lot of detail in the description.
3. Write about what happened to the main character after the story ended.
4. Write a new ending for the story.
5. Write a letter to the main character telling him/her how he/she could have handled the situation differently and what the result might have been.
6. Write a letter to the author telling the author what you particularly liked about the story.
7. Write a letter to the author suggesting a further adventure for the main character of the story.
8. Write a letter to the author suggesting a different ending to the story.
9. Write a diary or some journal entries for a character in the story.
10. Write a letter to a friend recommending the story.
11. Make a time line showing the events in the story.
12. Pretend to be a newspaper reporter. Write down five questions you would like to ask one of the characters in the story. After each question write the response you think the character might have given.
13. Explain what one of the characters would really like for dinner and tell why!
14. Explain what one of the characters would really like for a birthday present and tell why.
15. Draw a picture of one of the characters in the story and tell something about the character in your drawing.
16. Design a book cover for the story.
17. Create a poster about the story.
18. Write six questions about the story.
19. Make a bookmark for the story.
20. Write an advertisement about the story.
21. Write a newspaper style article about an event in the story.

22. Write six incomplete sentences about the story. Exchange sentences with another student and try to complete each other's sentences.

23. Fold a blank piece of duplicator paper in fourths or sixths. Number each block. Then draw pictures in sequence to depict happenings in the story. Write a short sentence at the bottom of each picture explaining what is shown in the picture.

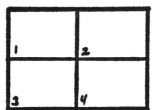 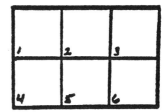

24. Select five interesting vocabulary words from the story and create a word study activity for those words. The activity could involve matching word with definition, a fill-in-the-blank activity, a crossword puzzle, a word-find puzzle, etc.

25. Write a story using all or almost all of the new vocabulary words in the story just read. Draw an illustration to go with your story.

CONSONANT CARS

(Grades 1–2)

PURPOSE: Reinforce initial consonant sounds and practice sounding out words

MATERIALS: —white tagboard or heavy white art paper
—black Flair pen
—watercolor felt-tip markers (assorted colors)
—Consonant Cars patterns
—photocopier or duplicator machine
—laminating materials
—scissors
—black dry-mark pen or black transparency pen
—box
—attractive contact paper
—black permanent ink felt-tip marker

PREPARATION: Duplicate or photocopy the Consonant Cars Pattern Page onto white tagboard or heavy white art paper to make 16–24 cars (the number to be determined by the attention span of the students). Color the cars with different colors of watercolor felt-tip markers. (Watercolor felt-tip markers will not soak through to the back of the tagboard or art paper cars; permanent felt-tip markers will.) Then use a black Flair pen to outline all of the lines on each of the cars.

Next select a number of three- or four-letter words that begin with a consonant and are at an appropriate reading level for the students. Omitting the initial consonant, print a different word on each car with the black Flair pen. Draw a line in front of each word to indicate a missing consonant. The students will fill in the missing consonant on this line. Examples of words, minus the initial consonants, that could be used on the cars include: __at, __ar, __an, __all, __et, __ell, __ig, __am, __ap, __ip, __ot, __ake, __ing, __ill, __ed, __eat, __ame, __ack, __en, __un, __ag, __it, __ide, __ate, __ent, __ad.

Laminate the cars. Then place the consonant cars in a box covered with attractive contact paper and print the activity title, CONSONANT CARS, on the top of the box.

PROCEDURE: Using a black transparency pen or a black dry-mark pen, have students individually or in pairs fill in the missing consonants on the cars to make real words. When the student or pair of students has completed filling in the missing consonants, check to see that real words have been formed and have the student(s) read to you some or all of the words that were made. Then wipe off the consonants written by the student(s) and the activity is ready for the next child or pair of children.

You will notice that more than one consonant can be filled in on each consonant car to form a real word. This means that students can do this activity over and over and still benefit from it because each time they will be forming many new words.

CONSONANT CARS PATTERN PAGE

TURTLES AND LOGS

(Grades 1–5)

PURPOSE: Match pairs of homonyns
    (*Variations*: Match capital and lower case letters, vowel sounds, synonyms, antonyms, rhyming words, contractions, or words to definitions)

MATERIALS: —large white index cards or white posterboard/railroad board
        —Turtle and Logs patterns
        —permanent Magic Markers (assorted colors)
        —black, permanent thin-line felt tip markers
        —scissors
        —laminating materials

PREPARATION: Using the Turtles and Logs Pattern Page, reproduce turtles and logs in quantity needed. Color turtles and logs with felt-tip markers. Laminate and cut out each piece. Using a black, thin-line permanent felt-tip marker, write one homonym of each homonym pair on the turtles and the corresponding homonyms on the logs. (See word lists at the end of the book.)

Note: This activity can be made self-correcting by writing a different numeral on the reverse side of each turtle and the same numeral on the reverse side of the log that matches the turtle. When a child has completed the activity, the turtles and logs can be turned over to see if the numerals on the reverse side of the matched turtles and logs are identical.

PROCEDURE: Have students match turtles to corresponding logs.

TURTLES AND LOGS PATTERN PAGE

SYNONYM SEARCH

(Grades 4–6)

PURPOSE: Vocabulary development and recognition of synonyms

MATERIALS: —unlined 5″ × 8″ yellow file cards
      —1 regular playing card
      —scissors
      —black Flair pen
      —laminating materials

PREPARATION: Using a regular playing card as a stencil, cut out 53 cards from yellow, unlined file cards. On one card, print the title SYNONYM SEARCH. This will serve as the game title card and will not actually be used in playing the game.

Next, select 26 pairs of synonyms appropriate for your students. The synonym pairs can be selected from the reading book and from other instructional materials, or can be selected from the list of synonyms provided at the end of this book. On each of the 52 cards, print a different word from those selected 26 pairs of synonyms. Print the same word on each end of the card so that no matter how the cards are shuffled, when spread out in the hand the words will be visible. (See the illustration.)

Next, make a Judge's Answer Key so students can check their pairs of synonyms while playing the game. Type the 26 pairs of synonyms onto an unlined 5″ × 8″, yellow file card. Type THE JUDGE'S ANSWER KEY at the top of the card.

Laminate the 53 cards and the Judge's Answer Key.

GAME DIRECTIONS: In this card game students try to match pairs of synonyms. Three to four players can play this game at a time. To play, shuffle the cards thoroughly, then deal out four cards to each player and place four cards face up in the center of the table.

The first player looks at the cards in his or her hand and the four cards turned up in the center of the table, trying to find pairs of synonyms that match each other. If the first player has a card in his or her hand that is the synonym of a card in the center of the table, he or she takes the card from his or her hand, says, "I am matching _____ with _____," picks up the card from the table and sets the matching pair face down in a pile beside him or her on the table.

If the first player has no card in his or her hand that is the synonym of a card in the center of the table, he or she must take one card from his or her hand and place it in the center of the table. It is then the next player's turn to try to match a card in his or her hand with a synonym card on the table. At any point, if a player is not quite certain whether two cards are synonyms, he or she can refer to the Judge's Answer Key. Or, if at any point another player questions whether two cards matched by a player really are synonyms, the Judge's Answer Key should be checked.

When all players have played all four cards in their hand, the dealer deals out four more cards to each player. Play continues in this manner until all cards in the players' hands have been used and there are no more cards to be dealt. The WINNER is the player with the most matched pairs of synonyms in his or her pile of cards.

Synonym Search
Judge's Answer Key

abrupt—sudden
ancient—old
bewildered—puzzled
bold—brave
capable—able
consider—think
create—make
drowsy—sleepy
expensive—costly
fascinating—interesting
frequently—often
hazardous—dangerous
irritated—mad

legend—story
miracle—wonder
miserable—unhappy
moist—damp
organize—arrange
precisely—exactly
preserve—save
quiver—shake
ridiculous—laughable
solemn—serious
terrified—frightened
tremendous—huge
urgent—important

WATERMELON FLASH CARDS

(Grades 1–6)

PURPOSE: To develop word recognition of new vocabulary words in the reading lesson

MATERIALS: —heavy white art paper or white tagboard
—red colored pencil
—green, washable felt-tip marker
—black, washable felt-tip marker
—Watermelon Flash Card patterns
—photocopier or duplicator machine
—laminating materials
—black transparency pen or black dry-mark pen

PREPARATION: Duplicate or photocopy the watermelon card patterns onto heavy white art paper or onto white tagboard. Using a washable, green felt-tip marker, color the watermelon rind areas on each of the duplicated watermelons. Next, color the interior of each watermelon lightly with a red colored pencil. Use a washable, black felt-tip marker to color each of the seeds. Then laminate and cut out each of the watermelon cards.

PROCEDURE: Using a black dry-mark pen or a transparency pen, print a different vocabulary word from the reading lesson on the back of each watermelon card.

Now you are ready to use the cards to introduce and drill on new vocabulary words in the reading lesson. First, introduce the new vocabulary words in the manner indicated in the teacher's manual for the basal reading program you are using. Then use the watermelon cards as fun flash cards to reinforce recognition of those new words.

When the instructional activity is completed, wipe off the words and write new words for the next reading group or for the next lesson.

Front   Back

WATERMELON CARDS PATTERN PAGE

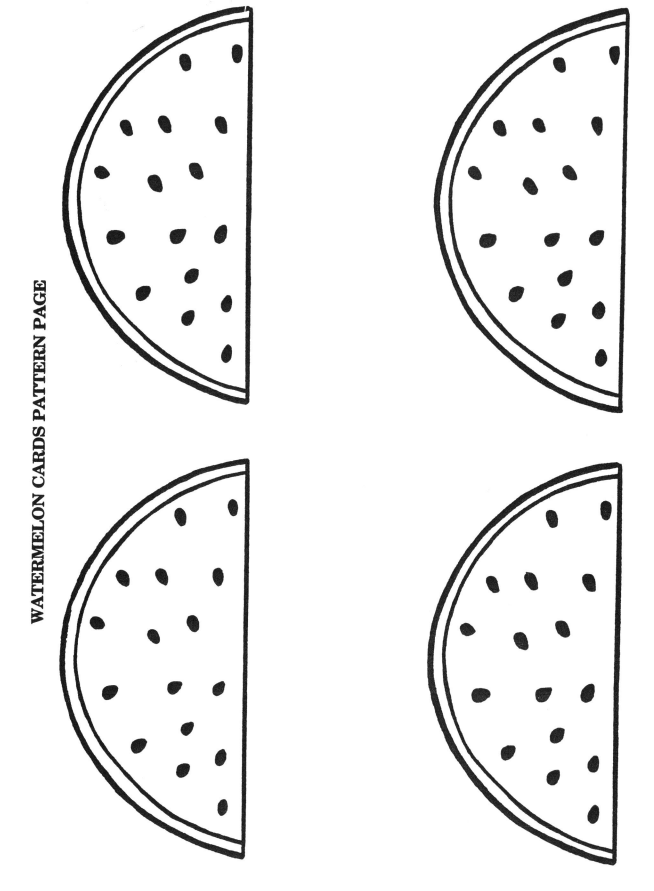

BONUS IDEA OF THE MONTH

PUFFED WORD FLASH CARDS

For students who have difficulty recognizing and retaining words being taught, try making puffed-word flash cards. A combination of the three-dimensional, textured, tactile character of these flash cards and the unique, dramatic attractiveness of these word cards results in words learned quickly and easily!

MATERIALS: —Paint Puffer*
  —acrylic paint (red, green, and blue)
  —$\frac{1}{4}''$ art paint brush
  —white tagboard or posterboard

* NOTE: Paint Puffer is a unique, non-toxic chemical formula which, when added to acrylic paint and heated, causes paint to expand to 50 times its original volume. Paint Puffer can be ordered from many of the large school supply companies. Or, it can be ordered from: V and W Distributors
  Watson Place
  Building 3-D
  Framingham, Massachussets 01701
  (Phone number: 1-800-365-1333)
  A 4-ounce bottle costs approximately $6.45

PREPARATION: Cut white tagboard or posterboard into flash cards, approximately 3″ × 5″ (3″ × 8″ if the words are long). Mix Paint Puffer with blue, red, or green acrylic paint, approximately two parts of paint to one part of Paint Puffer. Next, using an art paint brush, print sight words onto the flash cards with the paint/paint puffer mixture. The thickness of the paint film will determine the height of the puffed word. The thicker the film, the higher the puff. Dramatic results are obtained by building up layers. Therefore, apply several heavy coats of the paint mixture, letting each coat dry several minutes before adding the next coat.

The next step is to "puff" the words. The puffing occurs when heat is applied. The paint may be puffed when wet or dry. Heat a convection oven to 230° F. Put flash cards on a cookie sheet (in a single layer) and place in the oven. Dry paint will puff within seconds. Wet paint takes two to five minutes to puff. CAUTION: The puff will flatten out if the flash cards are left in the oven too long or if the oven temperature is too high (above 250° F).

(OTHER TIPS: The mixture of paint and paint puffer will keep indefinitely in a closed container. There is no time limit between painting and puffing. Apply the paint/puffer mixture to tagboard, railroad board, or posterboard. Thin paper may tend to curl during puffing.)

PROCEDURE: These attention-grabbing word recognition flash cards can be used for introducing vocabulary words to reading groups. Or, they can be used as tactile flash cards to build the sight word recognition of individual students with pronounced retention difficulty.

When used to teach words to students with severe reading disabilities, use the following procedure:

1. Show a word card to the student.
2. Tell the student the word.
3. Have the student say the word.
4. Have the student trace over the raised letters of the word with the index finger and middle finger of the hand with which the student writes.
5. Have the student repeat the word.
6. Have the student use the word in a sentence.
7. Have the student write the word on a sheet of paper, looking at the puffed word flash card as needed.

TEDDY BEAR TACHIST-O-SCOPE

(Grades 1–3)

PURPOSE: Recognize sight words
(*Variations*: Recognize letters, letter-sound relationships, compound words, rhyming words, etc.)

MATERIALS: —white railroad board or posterboard
—white tagboard or heavy white art paper
—Teddy Bear Tachist-o-Scope Pattern Page
—pencil
—black, fine-line marker
—permanent felt-tip markers—assorted colors
—colored pencils—assorted colors (optional)
—scissors
—tracing paper
—carbon paper
—laminating materials
—art knife
—washable transparency pen or dry-mark pen

PREPARATION: Trace the Teddy Bear Tachist-o-Scope pattern onto a sheet of tracing paper. Place the tracing paper on top of a sheet of carbon paper. Place these on top of a piece of white railroad board or posterboard. Trace over the tracing to transfer the teddy bear drawing on the tracing paper to the railroad board. Remove the tracing paper and carbon paper. Use a black, fine-line pen and/or black, felt-tip pen to outline the drawing. Color the teddy bear with a brown marker or with colored pencils. Color the bow on the teddy bear with a color of your choice. Cut out the teddy bear and laminate. Trim the laminating film from the cut-out. Using the art knife, cut two horizontal slots, approximately $2\frac{3}{4}''$ long and $1''$ apart, on the teddy bear's chest/stomach. Cut the tagboard or art paper into strips $2'' \times 11''$ and laminate.

PROCEDURE: Select sight words for practice in a reading group. Using a washable transparency pen or dry marking pen, print the sight words on the laminated plastic strip, one beneath the other and approximately $1''$ apart. Put the word strip behind the Teddy Bear Tachist-o-Scope and thread it through the bottom slot, then back through the top slot.

To use, slide the word strip up exposing a word. Call on a student to read the word. Then pull the word strip up to expose the next word and call on another student to read the word. Continue in this manner.

When finished with the sight word practice on the Teddy Bear Tachist-o-Scope, simply remove the word strip and wipe off the words with a damp paper towel. New words can be written on the word strip and the Teddy Bear Tachist-o-Scope is ready for use with the next reading group.

TEDDY BEAR TACHIST-O-SCOPE PATTERN PAGE

Motivation Book Report Form

THE COUNTDOWN TO A GOOD BOOK
(Grades 4–6)

Distribute a copy of THE COUNTDOWN TO A GOOD BOOK to each student. After students have finished reading a library book, have them write a book report on this motivation book report form. Have them begin at the bottom of the page with the title of the book and work up the page, filling in their book report information. When they have finished filling in the book report information, have them decorate and color-in the rocketship.

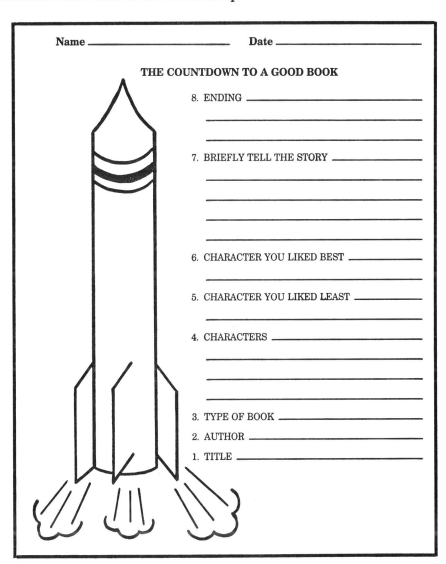

Name _____ Date _____

THE COUNTDOWN TO A GOOD BOOK

8. ENDING _____

7. BRIEFLY TELL THE STORY _____

6. CHARACTER YOU LIKED BEST _____

5. CHARACTER YOU LIKED LEAST _____

4. CHARACTERS _____

3. TYPE OF BOOK _____

2. AUTHOR _____

1. TITLE _____

THE COUNTDOWN TO A GOOD BOOK

8. ENDING ——————————————

————————————————————

————————————————————

7. BRIEFLY TELL THE STORY ——————

————————————————————

————————————————————

————————————————————

————————————————————

————————————————————

6. CHARACTER YOU LIKED BEST ————

————————————————————

5. CHARACTER YOU LIKED LEAST ————

————————————————————

4. CHARACTERS ————————————

————————————————————

————————————————————

————————————————————

3. TYPE OF BOOK ——————————

2. AUTHOR ———————————————

1. TITLE —————————————————

Motivation Book Report Form

A SQUARE BOOK REPORT
(Grades 4–6)

Distribute a copy of A SQUARE BOOK REPORT to each student. After students have finished reading a library book, have them write a brief book report on this motivational book report form. Have the students begin by filling in the title of the book and the author in the middle of the square. Next, you may wish to have them write a rough draft of what they want to tell about the book on another piece of paper. Then, after they have proofread and edited what they have written, they can copy the perfected version onto the book report form.

A SQUARE BOOK REPORT

Tell about the book:

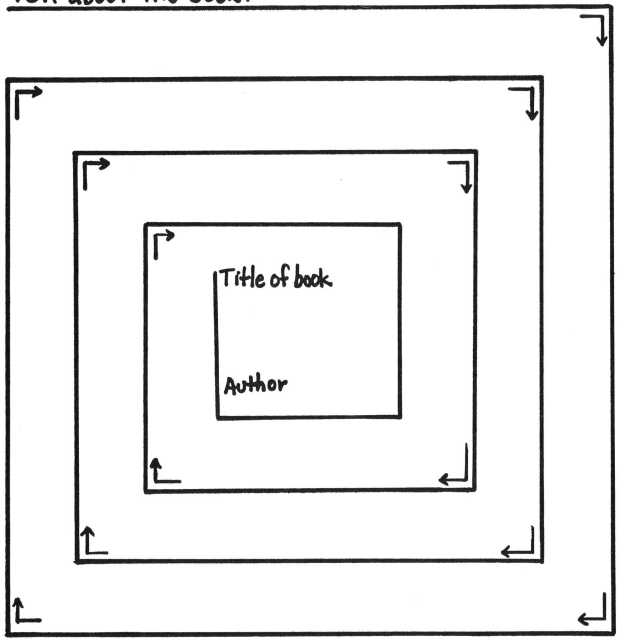

Title of book

Author

VOCABULARY PRACTICE TRANSPARENCY

Use this page to make a transparency for developing word recognition or for vocabulary/word meaning practice. Write the words to be practiced on the ice cream scoops with a washable transparency pen.

VOCABULARY PRACTICE TRANSPARENCY

Use this page to make a transparency for developing word recognition or for vocabulary/word meaning practice. Write the **words to be practiced** on the cards held by the teddy bears with a washable transparency pen.

Story Extension Activity

Name ______________________ **Date** ______________________

MY SUMMER VACATION WITH __________

Pick a character from one of your favorite stories. Imagine that this character spent two weeks of last summer vacation with you. Describe your two weeks together. Write an interesting story.

Title of Story ______________________________________

Author ______________________________________

Continue your story on another sheet of paper.

Story Extension Activity

Name _____   Date _____

CHARACTER PORTRAIT GALLERY

Select three characters from a story. Using crayons or colored pencils, draw a portrait of each. Beneath each portrait, write the name of the character and a description of what that character did in the story.

Title of Story _____

Author _____

Reading Motivation Bulletin Board

I CAN'T BEAR TO BE WITHOUT BOOKS!

(Grades 1–6)

PURPOSE: Reading motivation

MATERIALS: —yellow bulletin board paper

—bulletin board pattern

—permanent felt-tip markers (assorted colors)

—scissors

—stapler

—cut-out letters (optional)

PREPARATION: Cover a bulletin board with yellow bulletin board paper. Use an opaque projector to project the bulletin board pattern onto the bulletin board. Trace the picture onto the bulletin board paper with a black, felt-tip marker. Then color in the picture with appropriate colors of markers. Staple cut-out letters or trace the lettering to form the caption to complete the bulletin board.

NOTE: If an opaque projector is not available, make a transparency of the bulletin board pattern. Then, using an overhead projector, project the illustration onto the bulletin board paper to trace.

OPTIONAL (Primary grades only): Place a table in front of the bulletin board. Have the children bring teddy bears from home. Let each child place his/her teddy bear on the table or on the floor in front of the table. Then, let each child select a favorite book and place it with his/her teddy bear. The teddy bear can be positioned holding the book, sitting on the book, with the book set propped open in front of the bear, or in other interesting positions with the book. Cards with the children's names printed on them can be placed with the teddy bears, if desired.

I CAN'T BEAR TO BE WITHOUT BOOKS!

HALLOWEEN BOOKS FOR CHILDREN TO READ AND ENJOY

Below is a list of Halloween and Halloween-related books with *approximate* independent reading grade level indicated. These books can be displayed in a Halloween reading center. If you don't have space for a reading center display, display them along the chalkholder of the chalkboard. Talk them up to the students and encourage the children to read them, enjoy them, and share them with each other!

Most of these books are excellent for teachers to read aloud to children. The children will beg for more and more! When selecting books to read aloud, the reading grade level designations given below are not applicable since they indicate approximate student independent reading level.

Check with your school librarian or local public library children's librarian for the names of additional great Halloween-related books.

TRICKS FOR TREATS ON HALLOWEEN—Leonard Kessler	(1)
HENRIETTA'S HALLOWEEN—Syd Hoff	(1–2)
WHICH IS THE WITCH?—W. K. Jasner	(1–2)
HAUNTED HOUSES ON HALLOWEEN—Lillie Patterson	(1–2)
THE JACK O' LANTERN TRICK—Lillie Patterson	(1–2)
IT'S HALLOWEEN—Jack Prelutsky	(1–2)
THE SCARIEST WITCH IN WELLINGTON TOWERS— Joyce Segal	(1–2)
JACK THE BUM AND THE HALLOWEEN HANDOUT— Janet Schulman	(1–2)
ROTTEN RALPH'S TRICK OR TREAT—Jack Gantos	(1–2)
DINOSAUR'S HALLOWEEN—Liza Donnelly	(1–2)
SHAGGY DOG'S HALLOWEEN—Donald Charles	(1–2)
THE WITCH KITTEN—Ruth Carroll	(1–2)
HARRIET'S HALLOWEEN CANDY—Nancy Carlson	(1–2)
THE BIGGEST PUMPKIN EVER—Ruth Krauss and Crockett Johnson	(1–2)
HOW SPIDER SAVED HALLOWEEN—Robert Kraus	(1–2)
HALLOWEEN SURPRISES—Ann Schweninger	(1–2)
THE WITCH NEXT DOOR—Norman Birdwell	(1–2)
THE WITCH GROWS UP—Norman Birdwell	(1–2)
THE WITCH'S VACATION—Norman Birdwell	(1–2)
CLIFFORD'S HALLOWEEN—Norman Birdwell	(1–2)
TAFFY FINDS A HALLOWEEN WITCH—Donna Lugg Pape	(1–2)

HOBO DOG IN GHOST TOWN—Thacher Hurd   (1–2)

HALLOWEEN—Joyce Kessel   (1–3)

THE SPOOKY HALLOWEEN PARTY—Annabelle Prager   (1–3)

HOBBLE THE WITCH CAT—Mary Calhoun   (1–3)

GEORGIE—Robert Bright   (1–3)

GEORGIE'S HALLOWEEN—Robert Bright   (1–3)

GEORGIE AND THE ROBBERS—Robert Bright   (1–3)

A DARK, DARK TALE—Ruth Brown   (1–3)

HALLOWEEN WITH MORRIS AND BORIS—Bernard Wiseman   (1–3)

HALLOWEEN A B C—Eve Merriam   (1–3)

THE DRAGON HILL HALLOWEEN PARTY—Loreen Leedy   (2–3)

THE WITCH'S HAT—Tony Johnston   (2–3)

SPACE CASE—Edward Marshall   (2–3)

A HALLOWEEN MASK FOR MONSTER—Virginia Mueller   (2–3)

PUMPKIN, PUMPKIN—Jeanne Titherington   (2–3)

THE TERRIBLE HALLOWEEN NIGHT—James Stevenson   (2–3)

A TIGER CALLED THOMAS—Charlotte Zolotow   (2–3)

PLEASANT FIELDMOUSE'S HALLOWEEN PARTY—Jan Wahl   (2–3)

THE BERENSTAIN BEARS AND THE GHOST OF THE
    FOREST—Stan and Jan Berenstain   (2–3)

HALLOWEEN—Gail Gibbons   (2–3)

THE WITCH OF HISSING HILL—Mary Calhoun   (2–3)

ARTHUR'S HALLOWEEN—Marc Brown   (2–3)

HESTER—Byron Barton   (2–3)

HUMBUG WITCH—Lorna Balian   (2–3)

THE OLD WITCH AND THE GHOST PARADE—Ida DeLage   (2–3)

BEWARE! BEWARE! A WITCH WON'T SHARE—Ida DeLage   (2–3)

THE OLD WITCH AND THE SNORES—Ida DeLage   (2–3)

THE OLD WITCH GOES TO THE BALL—Ida DeLage   (2–3)

THE OLD WITCH AND THE GHOST PARADE—Ida DeLage   (2–3)

THE WITCH'S EGG—Madeline Edmondson   (2–4)

THE SO-SO CAT—Edith Thacher Hurd   (2–4)

THE SPOOK BOOK—Burton and Rita Marks   (2–4)

THE HAUNTING OF GRADE THREE—Grace Maccarone   (2–4)

THE HAUNTED HOUSE #3—Dorothy Haas   (2–4)

TOM LITTLE'S GREAT HALLOWEEN SCARE—John Peterson   (2–4)

FROM SEED TO JACK-O'-LANTERN—Hannah Lyons Johnson   (2–4)

TILLY WITCH—Don Freeman   (2–4)

THE VANISHING PUMPKIN—Tony Johnson   (2–4)

CRANBERRY HALLOWEEN—Wende and Harry Devlin   (2–4)

SIR WILLIAM AND THE PUMPKIN MONSTER—
    Margery Cuyler   (2–4)

SPOOKY AND THE WIZARD'S BATS—Natalie Savage Carlson   (2–4)

SCARY, SCARY HALLOWEEN—Eve Bunting (2–4)
THE WITCH WHO WAS AFRAID OF WITCHES—Alice Low (2–4)
THE LITTLEST WITCH—Jeanne Massey (2–4)
DORRIE AND THE HALLOWEEN PLOT—Patricia Coombs (2–4)
THE LITTLE LEFTOVER WITCH—Florence Laughlin (2–4)
THE BIGGEST PUMPKIN EVER—Steven Kroll (2–4)
MOUSEKIN'S GOLDEN HOUSE—Edna Miller (2–4)
TRICK OR TREAT—Lousi Slobodkin (2–4)
A WOGGLE OF WITCHES—Adrienne Adams (2–4)
THE LITTLE OLD LADY WHO WAS NOT AFRAID
OF ANYTHING—Linda Williams (2–4)
BATS AREN'T SWEET—Marilyn Jeffers Walton (2–4)
NO SUCH THING AS A WITCH—Ruth Chew (2–4)
THE WOULD BE WITCH—Ruth Chew (2–4)
THE WITCH AT THE WINDOW—Ruth Chew (2–4)
SUDDENLY A WITCH!—Irene Brown (3–5)
DANNY'S LUCK—Lavinia R. Davis (3–5)
THE HALLOWEEN PARTY—Lonzo Anderson (3–5)
WE CELEBRATE HALLOWE'EN—Bobbie Kalman (3–5)
HALLOWEEN TREATS—Carolyn Haywood (3–5)
HAUNTS AND TAUNTS—Jean Chapman (3–5)
SPOOKY STUFF—Shari Lewis (3–6)
A-HAUNTING WE WILL GO—Lee Bennett Hopkins (3–6)
IN THE WITCH'S KITCHEN: POEMS FOR HALLOWEEN—
Compiled by Brewton, Blackburn, and Blackburn (3–6)
HEY-HOW FOR HALLOWEEN—POEMS SELECTED BY LEE
BENNETT HOPKINS (3–6)
HALLOWEEN FUN—Judith Hoffman Corwin (3–6)
GHOSTS BENEATH OUR FEET—Betty Ren Wright (4–6)
CHRISTINA'S GHOST—Betty Ren Wright (4–6)
THE GHOSTMOBILE—Kathy Kennedy Tapp (4–6)
GHOST CAT—Beverly Butler (4–6)
MYSTERY OF THE WITCHES' BRIDGE—Barbee Oliver Carlton (4–6)
HAUNTED ISLAND—Joan Lowery Nixon (4–6)
13 GHOSTS—Will Osborne (4–6)
THE GHOST IN THE PICTURE—Meg Schneider (4–6)
THE NIGHT OF THE WEREWOLF—Franklin W. Dixon (4–6)
GHOSTS WHO WENT TO SCHOOL—Judith Spearing (4–6)
THE HAUNTING—Margaret Mahy (4–6)
WHICH WITCH?—Eva Ibbotson (4–6)
THE HANGMAN'S GHOST TRICK—Scott Corbet (4–6)
WITCHES, PUMPKINS, AND GRINNING GHOSTS—Edna Barth (4–6)
GHOSTS, WITCHES, AND THINGS LIKE THAT—Roderick Hunt (5–6)

EFFECTIVE INSTRUCTION TIP OF THE MONTH

STAMP OUT WANDERING MINDS:
OTHER GROUP PARTICIPATION TECHNIQUES

Hopefully you have begun using extensively the signaled responses described earlier in this book, and have also thought of many new signaled response activities to fit into your reading lessons. Now it is time to expand to some additional group response techniques. Again, these techniques are designed to help you keep students actively involved in the reading instructional activity—following along, thinking through the answer to *each* question, and actually answering each question. The more involved students are, the more reading skill development will take place!

Two additional types of group participation techniques you will want to employ extensively are *written response techniques* and *talk-it-over-with-a-buddy techniques*.

The first category is written response techniques. This could almost be considered a variation of signaled response techniques. The idea is to ask a question and, instead of calling on just one student to give an answer, have all students write their answers and then show you their answers. Here are several student-motivating methods for accomplishing this:

1. On individual-size chalkboards, have students write a response to your question. When you say, "Show me," all students hold up their chalkboards so that you can see their answers. Next, they erase their answers and are ready to answer the next question you beam to the group.

2. Laminate sheets of construction paper to make mark-on, wipe-off cards. Give one card to each student in the reading group. Then give each student a black, plastic marking crayon and a small rag. Beam a question to the whole group. Using the crayons, have the students write their individual responses on their laminated construction paper mark-on, wipe-off cards. Then have them hide their answers from the rest by turning their cards face down. When you say, "Show me," all students hold up their answers so you can see their individual responses. Students then wipe off their answers with their rags and are ready to write the answer to your next question.

   If you wish to make a game out of it, you can have students keep a tally of their correct answers. When the activity is completed, determine which student had the most tally marks. That student is the WINNER.

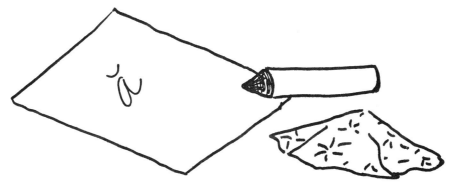

3. Have each student bring in an old sock and a round, plastic lid from a large coffee can or margarine tub. (Ask other teachers in your building to save large plastic lids so that you can supply them for students who do not bring lids.) Give each student a black, plastic marking crayon.

   The plastic lid is used as a substitute for or an alternative to the individual chalkboards or the laminated mark-on, wipe-off sheets of construction paper. Again, each student writes answers to questions you ask the group. Then, on your "Show me" statement, they show you their answers. Students then wipe off their answers with the old socks kept just for that purpose. When not in use, the plastic lids, socks, and plastic marking crayons can be kept in the students' desks.

The written response techniques using the individual chalkboards, the mark-on, wipe-off laminated cards, and the plastic lids work well for any type of activity in which you will be having students give short answers to your questions. Activities in which students write the vowel sound, consonant blend, consonant digraph, or number of syllables heard in a word, write synonyms, antonyms, or homonyms for given words, and identify prefixes, suffixes, root words, compound words, or rhyming words, will work well. Comprehension questions also can be asked as long as the answers are short answers.

The other type of group response technique is the talk-it-over-with-a-buddy technique. Here, instead of asking a question and calling on one student to answer, you ask the question and have pairs of students discuss their answers between themselves. Then you call on one of the groups to tell their answer. Here are some examples to get your ideas flowing:

1. In discussing the story the group has read, beam a comprehension question to the whole group. Ask them to silently think through their answers. Then ask them to turn to a person nearby and quietly discuss their answers together. After allowing sufficient time for the pairs of students to talk over their answers, call on one of the pairs of students to give their answer to the question. You may wish to ask the rest of the pairs to put "thumbs up" if they had the same answer or "thumbs down" if they had a different answer. If the answer given is correct, indicate that it is correct and briefly explain why or call on a student to briefly explain why. If it is incorrect, call on another pair of students to give their answer.

2. In discussing a story, beam a question to the whole group, have the students, in groups of two or three, discuss possible answers. After deciding on their answers, have each group write their answers on pieces of paper, fold the answers, and put them in an "Answer Box" placed in the middle of the reading group table. Next, reach into the Answer Box, mix the answers around, and draw one out. Read the answer aloud. Then have the students vote to indicate whether they agree or disagree with the answer. If the answer is incorrect, reach in the Answer Box and draw out another answer. Read it aloud and vote to determine agreement on the part of the rest of the class. If the students agree the answer is correct, call on a student to very briefly explain why that answer is correct.

The use of written response techniques and talk-it-over-with-a-buddy techniques is very effective in keeping students motivated and involved. Use these techniques often to stamp out wandering minds!

Multi-Purpose Gameboard

WITCH'S BREW
(Grades 1–6)

PURPOSE: Multi-purpose: letter recognition, letter sound relationships, sight word recognition, synonyms, antonyms, rhyming words, syllabication, definitions

MATERIALS: —14″ × 22″ sheet of orange railroad board or posterboard
—Witch's Brew gameboard
—permanent, black felt-tip marker
—scissors
—laminating materials
—game markers
—die

PREPARATION: Using an opaque projector, reproduce the gameboard on the 14″ × 22″ sheet of orange railroad board or posterboard with the black felt-tip marker. Print the game directions on the reverse side of the gameboard, if desired. Laminate the gameboard. With the permanent, black felt-tip marker, print different words or letters on each circle of the gameboard pathway depending on the skill the game is to reinforce.

You will also need three or four markers and a die.

NOTE: To change the words or letters on the laminated gameboard pathway, simply spray with hair spray and wipe off the words/letters with a tissue. The gameboard pathway will then be erased and ready for new words or letters again to be written on the laminated surface with permanent felt-tip marker. This simple technique makes it easy to change the skill being reinforced on the gameboard!

GAME DIRECTIONS: The game is played by two to four players. The object of the game is to take the witch to her pot of brew. The game markers are placed on the witch. The first player throws the die and moves a marker forward the indicated number of spaces, and performs the task (i.e., pronounces the word and says a synonym, names the vowel and says a word that contains that vowel, etc.) for the space upon which he/she has landed. If the player cannot perform the task, his/her marker must be moved back one space. It is then the next player's turn to throw the die, etc. The WINNER is the first player to land on the witch's pot of brew.

GHOST GAME

(Grades 2–6)

PURPOSE: Matching opposites

(Variations: matching capital with lower case letters, words beginning with the same consonant blends, synonyms, homonyms, etc.)
—½-yard, lightweight, white cotton fabric
—laminating film and machine
—black, permanent, fine-line felt-tip marker
—scissors
—1 sheet of tagboard
—ghost pattern

PREPARATION: Run white cotton fabric through the laminating machine just as you would a piece of posterboard. Trace the ghost pattern onto a piece of tagboard. Cut out the tagboard ghost to make a pattern to trace around. Place the pattern on the laminated fabric and trace around it with a black, permanent, fine-line felt-tip marker. Trace around the pattern to make a total of 36 ghosts. Using the marker, add eyes to each ghost. Then, cut out the ghosts.

On one side of a ghost, print a word. On another ghost, print an opposite. Continue in this manner, writing a word on one ghost and its corresponding opposite on another ghost to form 18 different pairs of opposites. (See lists at the end of the book for lists of opposites. Select pairs of opposites appropriate for the grade level.)

PROCEDURE: This game is played like the card game CONCENTRATION. Two or three students can play at a time. The students mix up the ghosts then spread them out in four rows of eight ghosts. The word side should be facing down.

The first player picks a ghost, turns it over, and reads the word on it. The player then picks a second ghost, turns it over, reads the word, and decides if it is the opposite of the first ghost picked. If the second ghost picked has a word that is the opposite of the word on the first ghost drawn, the player places the two ghosts on a pile beside himself/herself and then takes another turn. If the word on the second ghost is not the opposite of the word on the first ghost drawn, the player must return both ghosts, word side down, to the same places from which they were drawn. It is then the second player's turn to select two ghosts, trying to match opposites.

The game continues in this manner, with each player trying to remember what word was on each ghost and the position of each replaced ghost so that when he/she does draw the opposite for one of the words that has already been exposed, he/she will know exactly which card to turn over to match opposites.

Play continues in this way until all pairs of opposites have been matched. Each player then counts the ghosts in his or her pile. The WINNER is the player with the most ghosts.

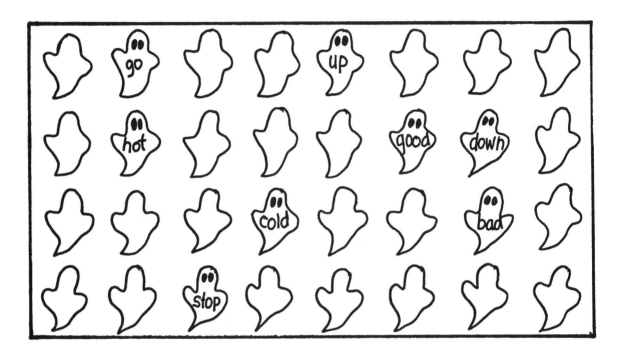

GHOST PATTERN PAGE

HAUNTED HOUSE GAME

(Grades 2–6)

PURPOSE: Recognizing number of syllables in words

(VARIATIONS: sight word recognition, letter recognition, letter-sound relationships, synonyms, antonyms, definitions, rhyming words, etc.)

MATERIALS: —14″ × 22″ sheet of orange railroad board or posterboard
—Haunted House gameboard
—permanent, black, felt-tip marker
—black, fine-line marker
—scissors
—oaktag or unlined file cards
—laminating materials
—game markers
—die

PREPARATION: Using an opaque projector, reproduce the gameboard on the 14″ × 22″ sheet of orange railroad board or posterboard with the black Magic Marker. Print the game directions on the reverse side of the gameboard, if desired.

Cut 2″ × 3″ cards from oaktag or unlined file cards. Select words from reading book or other words students will recognize. Print a different word on each card.

Laminate the gameboard and the cards.

You will also need three to four markers and a die.

GAME DIRECTIONS: The game is played by two to four players. The cards are shuffled and placed face down on the "Put Cards Here" box on the gameboard. The game markers are placed on the START block. The first player throws the die and moves a marker forward the indicated number of spaces, draws a card, pronounces the word, and says the number of syllables in the word. If the player cannot correctly indicate the number of syllables, he/she must move his/her marker back one place. It is then the next player's turn to throw the die, etc. The WINNER is the first player to land on the haunted house.

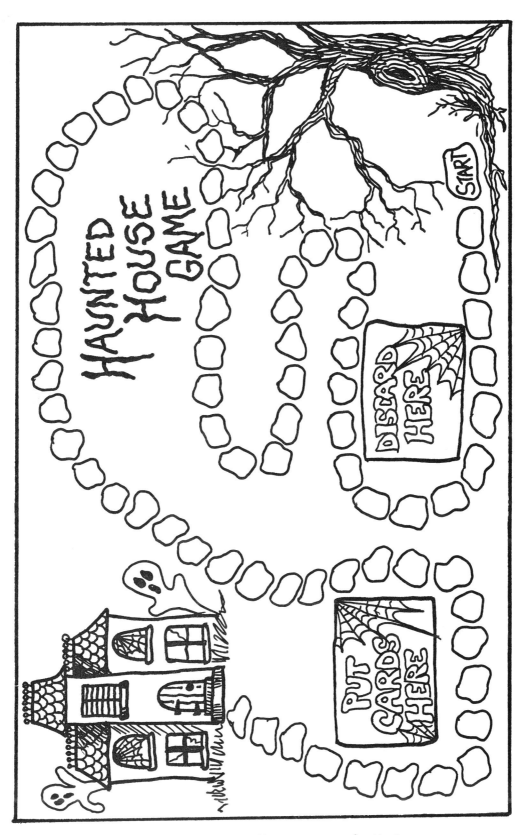

HAUNTED HOUSE GAME

START

DISCARD HERE

PUT CARDS HERE

CONSONANT BLEND CHECKERS

(Grades 2–4)

PURPOSE: Initial consonant blends

MATERIALS: —14″ × 14″ piece of yellow railroad board or posterboard
—permanent, black, felt-tip marker
—black, fine-line marking pen
—pencil
—yardstick
—laminating materials
—1 set of checkers

PREPARATION: Using a yardstick and a pencil, draw the checkerboard squares on to a 14″ × 14″ piece of yellow railroad board or posterboard. The checker squares should be 1½″ × 1½″. The gameboard border should be 1″ wide. Therefore, you will mark off 1″ then eight 1½″ intervals. This will form the borders and the eight 1½″ squares in each direction. With the black felt-tip pen, color in every other square, checkerboard style. Next, write a different consonant blend on each yellow gameboard square (see gameboard illustration).

You will also need a set of checkers. These can be taken from a regular checker game or they can be purchased separately, very inexpensively, at most toy stores.

PROCEDURE: Students play this game like regular checkers, except when a checker is moved on to a square, the player must say a word that begins with the consonant blend found on that square. If a player jumps a checker, he/she must name a word that begins with the consonant blend found on the square of the checker jumped as well as on the one landed upon.

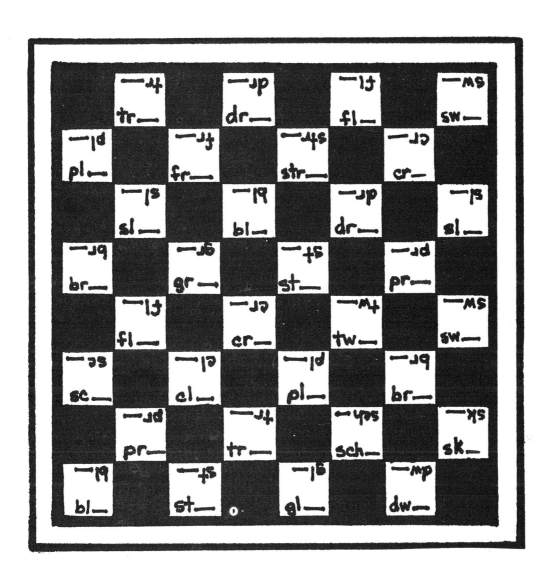

VOWEL VANS

(Grades 1–3)

PURPOSE: Reinforce short vowel sounds and practice sounding out words

MATERIALS: —pieces of railroad board (assorted colors or color of your choice)
- —Vowel Van pattern
- —black Flair pen
- —tracing paper
- —carbon paper
- —scissors
- —pencil
- —laminating materials
- —box
- —attractive self-stick vinyl
- —black dry-mark pen or black transparency pen

PREPARATION: Trace the Vowel Van pattern onto a sheet of tracing paper. Place the tracing paper on top of a sheet of carbon paper. Place these on top of a piece of colored railroad board. (Railroad board is simply posterboard that is colored on both sides.) Trace over the tracing to transfer the van drawing on the tracing paper to the railroad board. You will need 10–20 vans depending on the grade level and attention span of the students. Therefore, you will need to continue using the tracing paper and carbon-paper tracing technique to draw additional vans on assorted colors of railroad board. Next, use a black Flair pen to outline each of the vans on the railroad board. Then, cut out each van.

Now turn each of the Vowel Vans over so that the unmarked, reverse side is facing up. Next, select a number of three- or four-letter words, appropriate for the reading level of the group, that contain a short vowel. Print a different word on each van, omitting the vowel and drawing in its place a line long enough for a student to write in the missing vowel. Examples of words, minus the short vowel, that could be used on the vans include: f__ll, p__n, t__p, c__b, h__t, t__n, s__ck, b__g, w__nt, l__t, h__ll, d__d, b__ll, c__t, r__n, t__ll, b__g, s__t, th__n, w__n, c__t, f__n.

Laminate the Vowel Vans. Then place them in a box covered with attractive self-stick vinyl and print the activity title, VOWEL VANS, on the top of the box.

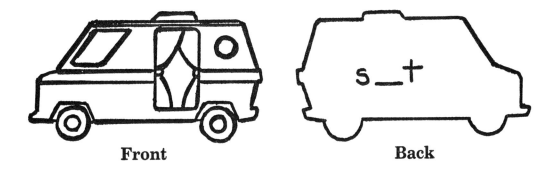

Front   **Back**

PROCEDURE: Using a black dry-mark pen or a black transparency pen, have students individually or in pairs fill in the missing vowels on the Vowel Vans to make real words. When the student or pair of students has completed filling in the missing vowels, check to see that real words have been formed and have the student(s) sound out some or all of the words that were made. Then wipe off the vowels written by the student(s) and the activity is ready for the next child or pair of children.

You will notice that more than one vowel can be filled in on each Vowel Van to form a real word. This means that students can do this activity over and over and still benefit from the activity because each time they will be forming many new words.

VOWEL VAN PATTERN PAGE

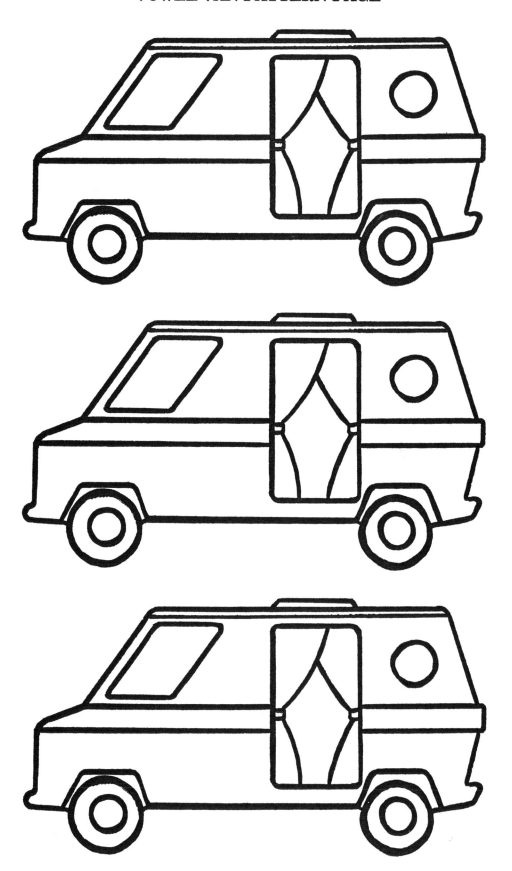

BONUS IDEA OF THE MONTH

A RECIPE FOR SPECIAL NON-ERASE CHALK

Here is a recipe for making a chalk that can be removed from a chalkboard only by wiping it off with a damp cloth! The possibilities for using this chalk are absolutely unlimited!

MATERIALS: 1 cup water
1 cup sugar
6 pieces of *soft* white chalk (the kind you buy in toy stores;
not school chalk)
pan
stove
waxed paper
Ziplock™ plastic bag

PREPARATION: Bring the water and sugar to a boil and stir. Remove the pan from the heat. Gently put the pieces of chalk into the hot sugar water solution and let them soak for 50 minutes. Then remove the chalk from the sugar water. Place the chalk on waxed paper and let dry overnight. Store the chalk in a Ziplock™ plastic bag.

(NOTE: When you write on the chalkboard with the non-erase chalk, the chalkmarks will first look dull and almost wet. In four or five seconds the chalk marks will "dry" full white.)

Examples of some ways to use the special NON-ERASE CHALK in CHALK-BOARD ACTIVITY CENTERS include:

1. WORDS AND DEFINITIONS (Grades 4–6)—Write definitions on the chalkboard with non-erase chalk. As an independent activity, have students come to the chalkboard to write the vocabulary word for each definition using regular chalk. When they erase their answers with an ordinary chalkboard eraser, the definitions written with the non-erase chalk

will remain, ready for the next student to write the corresponding vocabulary words. When you are ready to change the chalkboard activity, the definitions will wipe off easily with a damp cloth.

2. MAKING CONSONANT BLEND WORDS (Grades 1–3)—Write consonant blends on the chalkboard with non-erase chalk. The students, using regular chalk, apply phonics skills to create words containing the specified consonant blends. When they erase their words, using a regular chalkboard eraser, the consonant blends written with the non-erase chalk will remain, ready for the next student to do the chalkboard activity during independent activity time.

3. MARK THE SYLLABLES (Grades 5–6)—Write multi-syllable words on the chalkboard using the non-erase chalk. Students come to the chalkboard activity center singly or in pairs and, using regular chalk, divide each word into syllables applying rules of syllabification. When the activity is completed and checked by the teacher, by an assigned student "checker," or with an answer key, students erase their answers and the chalkboard activity center is ready for the next student(s).

4. ADD ROOT WORDS (Grades 3–6)—Write prefixes on the chalkboard using the non-erase chalk. A student adds root words to the prefixes, using regular chalk. After the student's work is checked, the student erases his or her words and the chalkboard activity center is ready for another student.

5. MARK THE VOWEL (Grades 1–2)—Print simple short and long vowel words on the chalkboard with the non-erase chalk. Using regular chalk, a student marks the vowels with long or short vowel marks. After the student's work is checked, the student erases the chalkboard to remove the vowel marks, and the activity center is ready for another student.

6. FILL IN THE VOWEL (Grades 1–2)—Using the non-erase chalk, print a number of one-syllable short vowel words on the chalkboard with the vowels omitted. Using regular chalk, a student writes in missing vowels to make real words. After the chalkboard activity is checked for accuracy and erased, the activity center is ready for another student.

The uses for the non-erase chalk at every grade level and in every subject area are unlimited! Put your imagination to work and create hundreds of fantastic applications for this "magic" chalk!

READING TAKE-HOME BAG

(Grades 1–2)

First- and second-grade students will eagerly await their turn to take home the READING TAKE-HOME BAG. This take-home bag also conveys to parents ideas of ways they can help their children gain reading skills!

PURPOSE: Reading motivation, reading reinforcement, parent involvement

MATERIALS: —canvas or denim tote bag (either purchased or handmade)
—permanent fabric marking pens—assorted colors (optional)
—material and sewing equipment (optional)
—picture books (for parents to read to child)
—easy library books (for children to read to parents)
—alphabet follow-the-dot book
—teacher-made or commercial high-interest reading readiness or reading instructional games
—an assortment of high-interest reading worksheets
—sight-word flash cards appropriate for the reading level of the students

PREPARATION: You will need to begin with a canvas or denim tote bag. If you are artistically inclined, you may wish to use fabric markers to print "READING TAKE-HOME BAG" across the top of the front panel and draw a large book beneath the lettering. If you have sewing ability, you may wish to appliqué the lettering and a book to the front of the tote bag. If your artistic ability and your sewing ability is limited, you can leave the tote bag unadorned.

Place two books in the Reading Take-Home Bag, one for the child to read to the parent and one for the parent to read to the child. Add a high-motivation, teacher-made or commercial reading readiness or reading skill developing game that the parent and child can play together. Then add a page from an alphabet follow-the-dot book, a couple of high-motivation reading worksheets, and a small pack of sight-word flash cards appropriate to the level of the child that will be taking home the tote bag on that day. And finally, include a letter to the parents briefly explaining the importance of the school and home working together to help their child learn to read and explaining the contents of the Reading Take-Home Bag and how to use each item.

And, last but not least, develop a chart listing students' names and indicating whose turn it is to take home the Reading Take-Home Bag. Post the chart on the wall where students can look at it to see when their turn will be coming.

PROCEDURE: The students take turns taking home the Reading Take-Home Bag for the evening and returning it the next morning.

To introduce the Reading Take-Home Bag to the students, show them the bag and enthusiastically explain that they will each get a chance to take it home overnight. Take the items out of the bag, one by one, and explain what each item is and what they are to do with it when they take the bag home. Explain that if their parents are not home in the evening to do the activities with them, they can do the activities with a babysitter, an older brother or sister, or a grandparent. Point out to them the chart on the wall showing who gets to take the bag home and when their turn will be coming. Then, look at the chart and announce the name of the first lucky child—the child who will get to take the bag home that evening. Be sure to explain that after each child in the class has taken the bag home once, you will put new items in the bag, and they will get to take it home again and again throughout the year.

Each morning, shortly after school begins, look at the chart indicating whose turn it is to take home the Reading Take-Home Bag. Announce the name of the lucky child and remind the child to be sure to get the bag at the end of the day. Then, at the end of the day, when the children are getting ready to leave, give the child the Reading Take-Home Bag. Be sure to remind the child to bring the bag back to school the next day. Then stand back and watch the beaming child leave the classroom proudly carrying home the bag!

After every child has taken the bag home, put new books, a new learning game, some new paper-and-pencil activities, etc., into the bag and let the children take turns taking it home again. Continue in this manner throughout the school year. The children and parents will love it!

HAUNTED HOUSE TACHIST-O-SCOPE

(Grades 4–6)

PURPOSE: Word recognition and vocabulary/word meaning

(Variations: basic sight word recognition, letter recognition, letter-sound relationships, rhyming words, synonyms, antonyms, etc.)

MATERIALS: —white railroad board or posterboard
—Haunted House Tachist-o-Scope Pattern Page
—white tagboard or heavy white art paper
—pencil
—black Flair pen
—permanent felt-tip markers—assorted colors
—colored pencils—assorted colors (optional)
—scissors
—tracing paper
—carbon paper
—laminating materials
—art knife
—washable transparency pen or dry-mark pen

PREPARATION: Trace the Haunted House Tachist-o-Scope pattern onto a sheet of tracing paper. Place the tracing paper on top of a sheet of carbon paper. Place these on top of a piece of white railroad board or posterboard. Trace over the tracing to transfer the haunted house drawing on the tracing paper to the railroad board. Remove the tracing paper and carbon paper. Use a black Flair pen to outline the drawing. Then, color the house using the Magic Markers and/or colored pencils. Cut out the haunted house and laminate. Trim the laminating film from the cut-out. Using the art knife, cut two horizontal slots, approximately $2\frac{3}{4}''$ long and $1''$ apart, on the haunted house. Cut the tagboard or art paper into strips $2'' \times 11''$ and laminate.

PROCEDURE: Using a washable transparency pen or a dry-mark pen, write Halloween-related words (see list below) on the laminated strips. Put a word strip behind the Haunted House Tachist-o-Scope, thread it through the bottom slot, and back through the top slot.

ghoul	flee	screech	grotesque
Halloween	horrifying	screams	mysterious
ghostly	frightening	wailing	disagreeable
ghastly	shriek	witches	disgusting
scary	costume	jack-o'-lantern	revolting
scared	pranks	cauldron	imagination

terrified	spooky	cemetery	skull
weird	skeleton	tombstone	spiders
peculiar	howl	gravestone	bats
odd	yowl	grave	ghosts

To use, slide a word strip up exposing a Halloween word. Have a student read the word and use it in a sentence or read the word and tell what it means. Then pull the word strip to expose the next word and call on another student to read the word and use it in a sentence or tell its meaning. Continue in this manner.

When students have finished reading all of the Halloween words on one strip, insert another strip with additional Halloween words and continue the activity. When finished, lay the Haunted House Tachist-o-Scope with the Halloween word strips in a convenient location where students can use it as a source of good Halloween words for writing Halloween stories.

HAUNTED HOUSE TACHIST-O-SCOPE

Motivation Book Report Form

GHOSTS AND SPOOKS

(Grades 2–6)

Display an assortment of Halloween-related books on a table in the classroom or along the chalkholder of the chalkboard. A listing of some Halloween books is found in this section of the book. Your school librarian or the children's librarian at your local public library can also help you select Halloween books your students will enjoy.

Point out to your students that Halloween is approaching. Tell them that you would like them to select a library book to read that seems especially appropriate for Halloween time. The book might be a story having a witch or a ghost in it. Or, it might be a story that takes place at Halloween.

Distribute a copy of GHOSTS AND SPOOKS motivation book report form to each student. Tell them that after they have finished reading a book they are to write a book report on this book report form.

The completed book report forms can be displayed on a wall or a bulletin board. Students can read each other's book reports and select additional books to read based on those reports.

Name _____ Date _____

GHOSTS AND SPOOKS

TITLE   AUTHOR   ILLUSTRATOR

Tell about the book. _____

Name _____ **Date** _____

GHOSTS AND SPOOKS

TITLE AUTHOR ILLUSTRATOR

Tell about the book. _____

_____

_____

_____

_____

_____

_____

_____

_____

_____

_____

_____

_____

_____

_____

_____

Motivation Book Report Form

IT WAS ENOUGH TO GIVE YOU NIGHTMARES!
(Grades 3–6)

Place copies of the activity sheet IT WAS ENOUGH TO GIVE YOU NIGHT-MARES! on a bookcase or on a book display table. Explain to the students that when they read a scary book of some type, whether it is a ghost story, or a mystery, or some other type of scary book, they should tell about it on this book report form.

You may also wish to have students turn the activity sheet over when they have finished filling it in and draw a picture of the scariest part in the book. Beneath their picture, they can write a sentence or two telling what is happening in the scene they have drawn.

Name _____   Date _____

IT WAS ENOUGH TO GIVE YOU NIGHTMARES!

Title _____

Author _____

Tell the story briefly. _____

_____

_____

_____

_____

_____

Which part was the scariest? _____

_____

_____

What else could cause nightmares? _____

_____

Why did you choose this book to read? _____

Would you recommend this book be read by others? _____

Name one person you think should read this book. _____

Name ——————————————— **Date** ———————————

IT WAS ENOUGH TO GIVE YOU NIGHTMARES!

Title ——————————————————————————————

Author —————————————————————————————

Tell the story briefly. ——————————————————————

————————————————————————————————————

————————————————————————————————————

Which part was the scariest? ————————————————————

————————————————————————————————————

What else could cause nightmares? ————————————————————

Why did you choose this book to read? ——————————————————

Would you recommend this book be read by others? —————————————

Name one person you think should read this book. ——————————

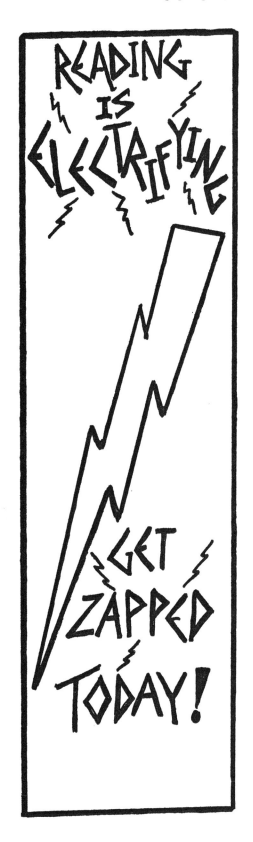

VOCABULARY PRACTICE TRANSPARENCY

Use this page to make a transparency for developing word recognition or for vocabulary/word meaning practice. Write the words to be practiced on the cauldrons with a washable transparency pen.

VOCABULARY PRACTICE TRANSPARENCY

Use this page to make a transparency for developing word recognition or for vocabulary/word meaning practice. Write the words to be practiced on the ghosts with a washable transparency pen.

Story Extension Activity

Name _____ Date _____

DESCRIBE THAT CHARACTER

Title of Story _____ Author _____

Select a character from the story. Write the name of the character on the line below. Then circle each word below that describes that character. Add additional descriptive words, if necessary. On the back of this page, explain why the descriptions you selected fit the character.

_____ Character's name

sad

bossy   thoughtful   quiet
                                                              shy
courageous
    disagreeable   intelligent
                    energetic
patriotic   honest   conceited
            curious   sad
sly   brave   messy   selfish
    gentle   studious   daring
                helpful   dreamer
                        nasty   considerate   short
dainty   adventurous   friendly   cooperative
    imaginative   handsome
                    serious   timid
unselfish   poor   lazy   mischievous
        bold   ambitious
    humorous   funny   responsible
                    cruel
            pretty

Story Extension Activity

Name —————— Date ——————

WHY DID YOU?

Choose 2 characters in a story and tell why each character acted as he or she did.

Title of Story ——————

Character: ——————

Character: ——————

Reading Motivation Bulletin Board

BULLETIN BOARD: BOOKS ARE SPELLBINDING

(Grades 1–6)

PURPOSE: Reading motivation

MATERIALS: —white or yellow bulletin board paper
—bulletin board pattern
—permanent felt-tip markers (assorted colors)
—colored pencils (assorted colors)
—scissors
—stapler

PREPARATION: Cover a bulletin board with white (or yellow) bulletin board paper. Use an opaque projector to project the pattern's lettering and picture onto the bulletin board. Trace the picture and lettering onto the bulletin board paper with a black felt-tip marker. Then color in the letters and the picture with appropriate colors of markers and colored pencils.

THANKSGIVING BOOKS FOR CHILDREN TO READ AND ENJOY

Below is a list of Thanksgiving and Thanksgiving-related books with approximate independent reading grade levels indicated. Some of these books are books of Thanksgiving activities. Others are historical fact or historical fiction. Still others are purely fiction. Your school librarian or children's librarian at your local public library will be able to recommend additional excellent books for the Thanksgiving season.

You may wish to create a Thanksgiving reading center or simply display them along the chalkholder of your chalkboard. Many of these books are perfect for teachers to read aloud to the students. Keep in mind the grade level designations indicated are approximate student independent reading levels and do not apply to appropriate grade level for reading aloud to students.

SQUIRREL'S THANKSGIVING SURPRISE—Valerie Tripp	(1–2)
IT'S THANKSGIVING—Jack Prelutsky	(1–2)
MYSTERY AT MOUSE HOUSE—Norma Q. Hare	(1–2)
PILGRIM CHILDREN COME TO PLYMOUTH—Ida DeLage	(1–2)
DON'T EAT TOO MUCH TURKEY—Miriam Cohen	(1–2)
SOMETIMES IT'S TURKEY—SOMETIMES IT'S FEATHERS— Lorna Balian	(2–3)
LITTLE BEAR'S THANKSGIVING—Janice	(2–3)
CHESTER CHIPMUNK'S THANKSGIVING—Barbara Williams	(2–4)
SQUANTO AND THE FIRST THANKSGIVING—Joyce K. Kessel and Lisa Donze	(2–4)
OUR THANKSGIVING BOOK—Jane Belk Moncure	(2–4)
THE THANKSGIVING MYSTERY—Joan Lowery Nixon	(2–4)
ARTHUR'S THANKSGIVING—Marc Brown	(2–4)
OVER THE RIVER AND THROUGH THE WOODS—Lydia Maria Child	(2–4)
THANKSGIVING DAY—Gail Gibbons	(2–4)
MOUSEKIN'S THANKSGIVING—Edna Miller	(2–4)
FARMER GOFF AND HIS TURKEY SAM—Brian Schatell	(2–4)
ONE TERRIFIC THANKSGIVING—Margorie Weinman Sharmat	(2–4)
FRIED FEATHERS FOR THANKSGIVING—James Stevenson	(2–4)
THANKSGIVING DAY—Robert Merrill Bartlett	(2–4)
LET'S FIND OUT ABOUT THANKSGIVING—Martha and Charles Shapp	(2–4)

DISTRIBUTE THOSE QUESTIONS

Many times we call on those students with their hands up much more frequently than we do students who do not have their hands up. In fact, many times we simply do not call at all on students who do not have their hands up or who look as though they don't know the answer. We do this thinking that we are saving the student who does not know an answer the embarrassment of being called on. However, at the same time, many students soon discover that if they don't raise their hands, they won't be called on, and, therefore, they don't have to pay attention. By not calling on all students, we are unintentionally conveying to students that they don't have to pay attention, they don't have to think through answers, they don't have to participate.

With that in mind, we need to use techniques that distribute our questions in ways that convey to each child, "You had better pay attention, you had better think through answers because you can and will be called on to answer questions whether or not you have your hand up." To do this we need to make sure that we are calling on every child in the reading group, whether or not they have their hands up and are looking eager to answer. We also need to use techniques that say to children that, just because you have been called on, doesn't mean that you won't be called on again.

The key is making sure we call on every student using a random pattern so that the students cannot predict ahead of time when their turn will be. Some ways of doing this include:

1. Write the names of the students in a reading group on file cards, one name per file card. Ask a reading lesson question, beaming it to all of the children in the reading group. Shuffle the file cards, then call on the student whose name is on the top, to answer the question. If that student cannot answer the question, call on the student whose name is on the next file card to answer the question. After a student has been called on, put his/her name card back somewhere in the pack of cards but not always at the bottom of the pack. Follow a similar procedure for the rest of the questions for the reading lesson, asking the questions, pausing, then calling on the student whose name comes up next on the file cards.

Be sure to hold the file cards so that students cannot see whose name is on the next card. We want each student thinking, "It might be me." Every so often, shuffle the file cards so that a student who has already been called on can be called on again and again if his or her name just happens to appear again and again. When you use this technique, students quickly realize that they will be called on whether or not they raise their hands, so they had better pay attention. They also quickly realize that they cannot "tune out" after they have answered a question because they may be asked another question.

> *NOTE*: You will need a separate set of name file cards for each reading group. Use this technique frequently with your reading groups.

2. Write the names of students in a reading group on Popsicle™ sticks (or tongue depressors). Cover an empty frozen juice can with attractive self-stick vinyl. Place the Popsicle™ sticks into the decorated can with the name ends down so that the names cannot be seen. Prepare a separate set of Popsicle™ sticks and decorated can for each reading group.

Ask a reading lesson question to the whole reading group, pause a couple of seconds to allow think time, then pull a Popsicle™ stick out of

the container and call on the student whose name is on the Popsicle™ stick to answer the question. If that student answers the question correctly, put the name stick back into the can. Ask another reading lesson question, pause a couple of seconds, draw out another name stick and call on that student to answer the question. If a student does not know the answer to the question, set his/her name stick down, pull another Popsicle™ stick from the container, and call on the student whose name is on that stick to answer the question. After that student answers the question correctly, indicate the answer is correct. Then ask the same question again to the student who could not answer correctly the first time. Expect that student to now be able to answer the question correctly because he/she just heard the correct answer given. Then place both name sticks back into the container and continue with the reading lesson, asking questions, and using the name sticks to determine who will be called on to actually answer the question.

Hints to maximize effectiveness of the technique:

a. Each time you put a name stick back in the container, try to put it in a different spot than the one previously put back into the container.

b. During the lesson, every so often casually mix the name sticks around in the container. That way, if you are unconsciously drawing most of the sticks from the front of the container, you will outwit the student who has already been called on, saw you put his/her name stick at the back of the can, and thinks you probably won't call on him or her again and therefore thinks it is safe to daydream or fool around.

c. After you ask a reading lesson question to the whole reading group, be sure to pause several seconds to allow time for *all* students to have to think through the answer. *Then*, draw a name stick out and call on the student to answer the question.

3. Write the names of the students in a reading group on small pieces of paper, one name per piece of paper. Fold each name paper once. You will

also need a hat of some type. It can be a cardboard hat of the type sometimes seen at parties or celebrations, a man's hat, a baseball cap, or even a football helmet. Place the folded name papers for the reading group you will be working with into the hat and mix the names around.

When discussing the story or working on a skills lesson, ask a lesson question to the whole reading group, pause several seconds to allow time for all students to think of an answer, then reach into the hat and draw a name out and call on that student to answer the question. After the student answers the question, fold the name paper back up again, put it back into the hat, and mix around all of the names in the hat. Continue using this procedure, asking a lesson question to the whole group, allowing think time, drawing a name out of the hat, calling on that student to give the answer, then returning the name to the hat and mixing around all of the names in the hat.

One of these techniques, or a similar technique that you may think of, should be used almost daily to make sure that you are calling on all students, not just the ones with their hands up. Frequent use of these techniques conveys to each of the students that they must pay attention, they must think through each answer, and just because they have already been called on doesn't mean they won't be called on again. Implementing these simple questioning techniques results in a high degree of student involvement, student thinking, and student reading skill development during the lesson!

Multi-Purpose Gameboard

TURKEY CHASE

(Grades 1–6)

PURPOSE: Multi-purpose: letter recognition, letter sound relationships, sight word recognition, synonyms, antonyms, rhyming words

MATERIALS: —14″ × 22″ sheet of brown railroad board or posterboard
  —Turkey Chase gameboard
  —permanent, black felt-tip marker
  —colored pencils
  —scissors
  —oaktag or unlined file cards
  —laminating materials
  —game markers
  —die

PREPARATION: Using an opaque projector, reproduce the gameboard on the 14″ × 22″ sheet of brown railroad board or posterboard with black felt-tip marker. Use colored pencils to add color to the Pilgrim boy and to the turkey. Print the game directions on the reverse side of the gameboard, if desired.

Cut 2″ × 3″ cards from oaktag or unlined file cards. Print different words or letters on each card depending on the skill the game is to reinforce.

Laminate the gameboard and the cards.

You will also need three or four markers and a die.

GAME DIRECTIONS: The game is played by two to four players. The cards are shuffled and placed face down on the "Put Cards Here" box. The game markers are placed on the Pilgrim. The first player throws the die and moves a marker forward the indicated number of spaces, draws a card, and performs the task (i.e., pronounces the word and gives its meaning, pronounces the word and says an opposite, or names the letter and tells a word that begins with the letter, etc.) If the player cannot perform the task, he/she must move his/her marker back one place. It is then the next player's turn to throw the die, etc. The WINNER is the first player to land on the turkey.

FIX-UM TEPEES

(Grades 2–6)

PURPOSE: Use of context clues

MATERIALS: —light brown construction paper
—Fix-Um Tepee patterns
—Manila envelope or decorative wallpaper envelope
—colored pencils (assorted colors)
—black Flair pen
—permanent, black felt-tip marker
—rubber cement
—scissors
—photocopier or duplicator machine
—laminating materials
—X-Acto™ Knife or single-edge razor blade
—black dry-mark pen or black transparency pen

PREPARATION: Photocopy or duplicate the Fix-Um Tepee Pattern Page onto light brown construction paper to make 12–16 tepees. The actual number of Fix-Um Tepees you make should depend on the grade level/attention span of the students. Use a black Flair pen to outline the border and markings on each tepee. Use orange-, yellow-, red-, blue-, and green-colored pencils to color the markings on the tepees. Cut out each tepee. Use rubber cement to glue one tepee on the front of a Manila envelope. Using a permanent, black felt-tip marker, print the activity title, FIX-UM TEPEES, on the front of the envelope. On the back of the envelope write the following directions:

Fix the tepees.

1. Read the sentences on the tepees.
2. Using the marking pen, fill in the missing words so that sentences make sense.
3. When you have finished, write the sentences you have made on a sheet of notebook paper and put the paper on the teacher's desk.
4. Then wipe off the words you wrote on the tepees and put the tepees back in the envelope.

Write a different sentence on the back of each tepee, omitting one word in each sentence and drawing a line in its place. The line should be long enough for students to write or print a word of their choice that would make sense. You can make up the sentences for the activity, or select them from the reading textbook, or select sentences at an appropriate level of difficulty from the context clue sentences provided at the back of this book.

Laminate the tepees and the activity envelope. Cut the tepees and the envelope out of the laminating film. Carefully slit the envelope opening with an X-Acto™ Knife. Fold down and crease the envelope flap. Place the Fix-Um Tepees in the activity envelope.

A black dry-mark pen or a washable black transparency pen will also be needed for the activity.

PROCEDURE: This activity is an independent activity. The students read the sentence on the back of a tepee, noting the missing word in the sentence. They use context clues to determine a word that would make sense in the sentence. Then, using a black dry-mark pen or a washable transparency pen, they fill in the word on the blank on the Fix-Um Tepee card. When each tepee has been "fixed" in this manner, the student should neatly write each of the sentences he or she has created on a sheet of notebook paper and place the paper on the teacher's desk for the teacher to check at a convenient time. The student should then wipe the words off the blanks on the tepees and put the tepees back in the envelope. The activity is then ready for the next student.

Front   **Back**

FIX-UM TEPEES PATTERN PAGE

SORT THE GINGERBREAD BOYS
(Grades 3–6)

PURPOSE: Auditory discrimination of hard and soft *g*

MATERIALS: —14″ × 22″ piece of colored railroad board or posterboard
—Gingerbread Boys patterns
—paper cutter
—light-brown construction paper
—permanent, black felt-tip marker
—black Flair Pen (or similar fine-line marker)
—white-colored pencil
—duplicator machine
—two 9″ × 12″ Manila envelopes
—rubber cement
—bookbinding tape
—X-Acto™ Knife
—laminating materials
—box
—attractive self-stick vinyl

PREPARATION: Cut a 14″ × 22″ piece of colored railroad board or posterboard into two pieces, 14″ × 11″ in size. Place the two pieces of posterboard side-by-side with approximately a ⅛″ gap between the two pieces. Tape the two pieces together with bookbinding tape. The tiny space between the two pieces will allow the activity board to fold easily along the seam. Now, print the title, SORT THE GINGERBREAD BOYS, across the top of the two pieces of posterboard with the black, permanent ink felt-tip marker. Next, cut the tops off of the 9″ × 12″ Manila envelopes to make them 9″ × 10″. Glue the two envelopes onto the posterboard.

Duplicate the gingerbread boy patterns onto light-brown construction paper to make 20–30 gingerbread boys. Use the black Flair Pen to outline all of the lines on the gingerbread boys. Color in the eyes, nose, mouth, buttons, and the icing lines on the arms and legs with white-colored pencils. Then select words appropriate for the reading level of the students from the list of hard and soft *g* words provided at the back of this book. Print a different word on each gingerbread boy. Then cut out each of the gingerbread boys.

Print HARD G on one Manila envelope on the activity board. Print SOFT G on the other Manila envelope. Select two of the gingerbread boys, one with a hard *g* word and one with a soft *g* word and glue each one onto the front of the matching Manila envelope.

Laminate the activity board and all of the remaining gingerbread boys. Use an X-Acto™ knife to slit open the tops of the Manila envelopes. Place the gingerbread boys in a box covered with attractive self-stick vinyl. The activity center is now ready for student use.

PROCEDURE: Students sort the gingerbread boys into the correct envelope on the activity board according to whether the word has a soft *g* or a hard *g*.

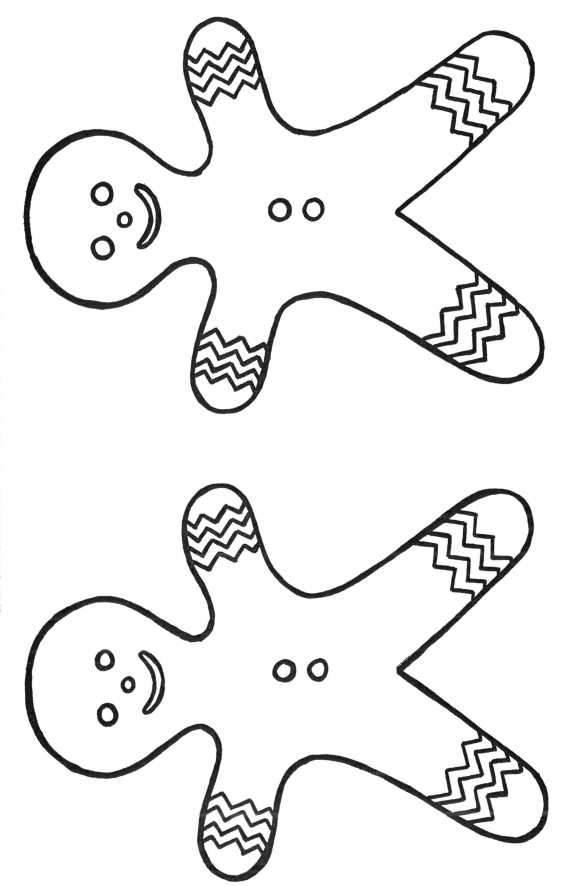

AN ESSENTIAL DICTIONARY SKILL
(Grades 3–6)

Students in grades 3–6 need direct instruction on how to look up in a dictionary the correct spelling of a word they don't know how to spell. Think of the times students have asked you how to spell a word and you have sent them to the dictionary to look up the spelling. The problem is, for many of these students, finding in a dictionary a word they don't know how to spell is an impossible task. Often, they only know how to find a word they already know how to spell.

Think about the dictionary skills instruction we provide students. It almost entirely involves locating words for which the spelling is provided. No wonder, then, that students are stymied when it comes to looking up a word they don't know how to spell. If we want students to be able to use a dictionary to determine the correct spelling of a word, we must teach them how to do it!

Procedure for Teaching Students How to Find the Correct
Spelling of a Word in the Dictionary

MATERIALS: dictionaries
                paper and pencils

PREPARATION: Select several words the students will probably not know how to spell automatically. These words should be in the students' reading and word meaning vocabulary, but not in their spelling vocabulary.

PROCEDURE: Provide each student with a dictionary, a piece of notebook paper, and a pencil. Tell students that they are going to learn how to use a dictionary to find the correct spelling of a word they don't know how to spell. Explain that this is probably the most essential and useful dictionary skill they will ever learn.

Explain that, when they wish to find the correct spelling of a word in the dictionary, they should use the following procedure:

1. Pronounce the word softly to yourself.
2. Guess some possible spellings based on the sounds heard in the word.
3. Write down three possible spellings.
4. Look up your first guess of a possible spelling in the dictionary.
5. If you find a word spelled that way in the dictionary, quickly check the definition to make sure you have the right word.
6. If you cannot find a word spelled that way in the dictionary, look in the dictionary for a word with your second possible spelling guess. If you find a word with that spelling, check the definition to make sure it is the right word.

7. If you still have not found the right spelling in the dictionary, try the third possible spelling.
8. If you still can't find the word in the dictionary, write down some more possible spellings and look them up, one by one. Or, glance down through the dictionary entries in the area of your spelling guesses and see if you can find the word you are looking for.

After explaining the procedure to the students, provide guided practice. Pronounce a word and ask them to find the correct spelling of that word in their dictionaries. Have them begin by jotting down three possible spellings on paper. Then have them look up the possible spellings, one by one, in the dictionary until they locate the correct spelling.

Have students point to the word in the dictionary and raise their other hand when they have located the correct spelling. As hands are raised, move around the room checking students' answers. Follow the same procedure with several more practice words.

To make sure the skill is learned and becomes automatic, this activity should be used every few days for several weeks. Students will enjoy the activity and will quickly develop an essential dictionary skill.

BONUS IDEA OF THE MONTH

MULTI-SENSORY FLASH CARDS

For children in first and second grades and remedial reading, these multi-sensory flash cards can be both fun to use and effective in helping children retain words being taught. These flash cards appeal to the sense of smell, as well as the visual and tactile/kinesethetic modes.

MATERIALS: —box of gelatin mix
  —white school glue
  —a school-type paintbrush, ½″ wide
  —sheets of white tagboard
  —1 paper or styrofoam cup
  —paper cutter

PREPARATION: Cut white tagboard into flash cards, approximately 3″ × 8″. Select words you wish to use on the flash cards. Pour approximately ½ of a cup of white school glue into a paper or styrofoam cup. Next, dip the paintbrush into the glue and print the first word on a card, using a generous amount of glue. Next, sprinkle powdered gelatin generously over the wet glue. Set the card off to the side to dry. Continue using the same procedure for the remaining word cards you wish to make. Let the cards dry overnight. Shake off the excess gelatin and the multi-sensory flash cards are ready to use.

PROCEDURE: These flash cards can be used for introducing vocabulary words to reading groups. Or, they can be used as tactile flash cards to build word recognition for individual students with retention difficulty.

When used to teach words to students with severe reading difficulties, use the following procedure:

1. Show a word card to the student.
2. Tell the student the word.
3. Have the student say the word.

4. Have the student trace over the raised letters of the word with the index finger and middle finger of the hand with which the student writes.
5. Have the student repeat the word.
6. Have the student use the word in a sentence.
7. Have the student write the word on a sheet of paper, looking at the flash card as needed.

NOTE: Different sets of flash cards can be given different smells by sprinkling the glue letters with different flavors of gelatin. Flash cards with words that smell like raspberry, cherry, grape, strawberry, orange, lemon, or lime have lots of child appeal!

SKILL AWARD RIBBONS

(Grades 1–3)

PURPOSE: To motivate students to master designated basic sight words, consonants, consonant blends, short vowels, and/or long vowels

PROCEDURE: Are you searching for a way to motivate students to eagerly master a specific skill and to clamor to demonstrate their knowledge to you? Award ribbons for mastery of specific skills and you will be amazed how motivated your students will be!

First decide on the skill objective you want the students to master and how they are to demonstrate that mastery. Next, have a classroom quantity of blue ribbons indicating the skill printed by a local printing company. (Use the yellow pages of the telephone book to find a printing company. If the printer you call does not print ribbons, he will be able to tell you who does.) When you have the ribbons, show them to the students and explain exactly how they can earn one. Then, when individuals have mastered the target skill and proven that mastery to you, award an official blue ribbon for the accomplishment.

READING SIGHT WORDS • READING CONSONANTS • READING CONSONANT BLENDS • READING LONG VOWELS • READING SHORT VOWELS

GIVE THEM A MARKER

(Grades 1–4)

Some students have great difficulty reading because, as they complete a line of print and their eyes swing back and down to begin reading the next line, they accidentally skip a line of print. Other students with this type of difficulty may be reading along, and while reading the line of print their eyes may skip down to a word on the next line, and they continue reading on the wrong line. In either case, students with this type of problem will have trouble keeping their place when others are reading. They will also certainly have trouble making sense of what they are reading when every so often they skip a whole line or part of a line of print.

As you listen to students read aloud, it is very easy to identify the students who have difficulty staying on the correct line. Make a mental note of those students. Then, at an inconspicuous time, give each of those children a marker, and show them how to put it under a line of print and shift it down the page as they read. This will help them stay on the right line as they read.

While we usually think only of first graders using markers like this, students in second through fourth grade and even higher, who are having a perceptual problem that results in skipping lines while reading, should be encouraged to use a marker to help them stay on the correct line of print. There is nothing wrong with allowing these older children to use this "crutch." Indeed, we have a responsibility to provide children who are having difficulties with techniques that will allow them to become successful readers! Rest assured, when the child no longer needs a marker to focus on the right line, he or she will discontinue using it without any pushing from you.

GORILLA TACHIST-O-SCOPE

(Grades 1–6)

PURPOSE: Multi-purpose (letter sound relationships, synonyms, antonyms, rhyming words, sight word recognition, definitions, short or long vowel sounds, consonant blends, digraphs, prefixes or suffixes)

MATERIALS: white railroad board or posterboard
—Gorilla Tachist-o-Scope pattern
—white tagboard or heavy white art paper
—pencil
—black fine-line marker
—permanent felt-tip markers—assorted colors
—colored pencils—assorted colors
—scissors
—tracing paper
—carbon paper
—laminating material
—art knife
—washable transparency pen or dry-mark pen

PREPARATION: Trace the Gorilla Tachist-o-Scope pattern onto a sheet of tracing paper. Place the tracing paper on top of a sheet of carbon paper. Place these on top of a piece of white railroad board or posterboard. Trace over the tracing to transfer the gorilla drawing on the tracing paper to the railroad board. Remove the tracing paper and the carbon paper. Use a black fine-line pen to outline the drawing. Color the gorilla brown and his eyes blue. Cut out the gorilla and laminate. Trim the laminating film from the cut-out. Using the art knife, cut two horizontal slots, approximately $2\frac{3}{4}''$ long and $1''$ apart on the chest of the gorilla. Cut the tagboard or art paper into strips $2'' \times 11''$ and laminate.

PROCEDURE: Select vocabulary words for word recognition practice or word meaning development in a reading group lesson or phonics or word attack elements for direct instruction or practice, etc. Using a washable transparency pen or dry-mark pen, print the words, letters, or letter groupings on the laminated strip, one beneath the other and approximately $1''$ apart. Put the word strip behind the Gorilla Tachist-o-Scope and thread it through the bottom slot, then back through the top slot.

To use, slide the word strip up exposing a word, letter, or letter grouping and call on a student to read the word or give a word that has the phonics element indicated. Then pull the strip up to expose the next item and call on another student to answer. Continue in this manner.

When finished with the drill/practice lesson with the reading group, simply remove the word strip and wipe it off with a damp towel. New words or letters can then be written on the word strip and the Gorilla Tachist-o-Scope is ready for use with the next reading group.

GORILLA TACHIST-O-SCOPE

Motivation Book Report Form

DESIGN A BOOK REPORT
(Grades 4–6)

Distribute a copy of DESIGN A BOOK REPORT to each student. After students have finished reading a library book, have them write a book report on this motivational book report form. When they have filled in the information, they can lightly color the various sections with different colors of crayons or colored pencils. The completed book report forms can then be displayed for other students' viewing.

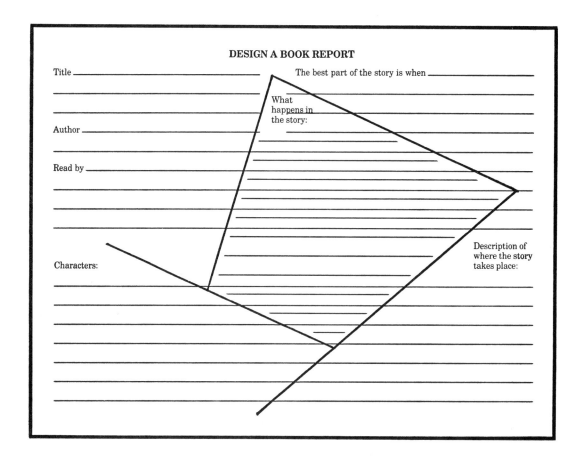

DESIGN A BOOK REPORT

The best part of the story is when

Title

Author

Read by

Characters:

What happens in the story:

Description of where the story takes place:

TIMES OF OLD

(Grades 3–6)

Ask students to select and read a book about historical people or events, or a book of historical fiction. (If students are not familiar with the difference between the two types of books, take time to explain the difference. Students may also need to be shown where the two types of books are found in the library.) Then distribute a copy of the activity sheet "Times of Old" to each student. After the students have finished reading the library book, have them write a book report on this activity sheet.

Optional Follow-Up Activity:

Designate a Times-of-Old Day. Ask each student to dress as a character from the book he or she has read. Then have them take turns standing up, holding their book and the activity sheet "Times of Old," and telling the rest of the class about the book. Have students limit the description of the book to not more than five or six sentences so that students will not get bored listening to long "book reports."

The activity sheets can then be displayed on a wall or bulletin board for further reference by students wishing to read each other's books.

TIMES OF OLD

Book title _____

Author _____

Type of book: HISTORY _____   HISTORICAL
                                    FICTION _____

Tell about the book. _____

_____

_____

_____

_____

_____

_____

Signature of reader _____

VOCABULARY PRACTICE TRANSPARENCY

Use this page to make a transparency for developing word recognition or for vocabulary/word meaning practice. Write the words to be practiced on the semi-trucks with a washable transparency pen.

VOCABULARY PRACTICE TRANSPARENCY

Use this page to make a transparency for developing word recognition or for vocabulary/word meaning practice. Write the words to be practiced on the cards held by the octopus with a washable transparency pen.

Name _____ **Date** _____

IT'S TIME TO GIVE THANKS

Title of story _____

Author _____

Make a list of things for which each character in the story should be thankful. Begin by writing the name of one of the story characters on a sheet of notebook paper. Think about the story, then beneath that character's name list a number of things for which that character should be thankful. Continue the same procedure for each of the other characters in the story.

When you have finished, staple this page to your page of lists to make a cover.

Story Extension Activity

Name —————————————— **Date** ——————————

FIRST . . . AND THEN

Title of story ————————— Author ——————

In box number 1, draw a picture showing how the story began. In box number 2, draw a picture showing how the story ended.

1	**2**

Reading Motivation Bulletin Board

BULLETIN BOARD: THREE CHEERS FOR BOOKS!
(Grades 1–6)

PURPOSE: Reading motivation
MATERIALS: —white bulletin board paper
 —bulletin board pattern
 —permanent felt-tip markers (assorted colors)
 —scissors
 —stapler
 —book covers (optional)
PROCEDURE: Cover a bulletin board with white bulletin board paper. Use an opaque projector to project the lettering and picture onto the bulletin board. Trace the picture and lettering onto the bulletin board paper with a black felt-tip marker. Then color in the letters and picture with appropriate colors of markers. OPTIONAL: Book covers of selected good books can be attached to the bulletin board, if desired.

NOTE: If an opaque projector is not available, make a transparency of the bulletin board picture. Then, using an overhead projector, project the illustration onto the bulletin board paper to trace.

Three Cheers for Books!

DECEMBER

HOLIDAY BOOKS FOR CHILDREN TO READ AND ENJOY

Below is a list of holiday books with approximate independent reading grade levels indicated. Some of these books are books of holiday activities. Others tell Biblical stories. Still others are purely fiction. Your school librarian or children's librarian at your local public library will be able to recommend additional excellent books for the holiday season.

You may wish to create a holiday reading center or simply display them along the chalkholder of your chalkboard. Many of these books are absolutely perfect for teachers to read aloud to students. Keep in mind the grade level designations indicated are approximate student independent reading levels and do not apply to an appropriate grade level for reading aloud to students.

CHRISTMAS SECRETS—Ann Schweninger	(1–2)
A BEAR FOR CHRISTMAS—Holly Keller	(1–2)
MAX'S CHRISTMAS—Rosemary Wells	(1–2)
MARMALADE'S CHRISTMAS PRESENT—Cindy Wheeler	(1–2)
TEDDY'S CHRISTMAS—Michelle Cartlidge	(1–2)
CHRISTMAS WITH THE BEARS—Susan J. Harrison	(1–2)
CLAUDE THE DOG—David Gackenbach	(1–2)
MERRY CHRISTMAS HENRIETTA—Sid Hoff	(1–2)
THE BEARS' CHRISTMAS—Stan and Jan Berenstain	(1–2)
TWELVE BELLS FOR SANTA—Crosby Bonsall	(1–2)
CHARLEY THE MOUSE FINDS CHRISTMAS—Wayne Carley	(1–2)
ARTHUR'S CHRISTMAS COOKIES—Lillian Hoban	(1–2)
THE MOUSES' TERRIBLE CHRISTMAS—True Kelley and Steven Lindblom	(1–2)
THE PERFECT CHRISTMAS PICTURE—Fran Manushkin	(1–2)
IT'S CHRISTMAS—Jack Prelutsky	(1–2)
THE HORRIBLE HOLIDAYS—Audrey Wood	(1–2)
CLIFFORD'S CHRISTMAS—Norman Bridwell	(1–3)
NO TIME FOR CHRISTMAS—Judy Delton	(1–3)
MERRY CHRISTMAS, AMELIA BEDELIA—Peggy Parish	(1–3)
THE BOY WHO WAITED FOR SANTA CLAUS—Robert Quackenbush	(1–3)
M&M AND THE SANTA SECRETS—Pat Ross	(1–3)
CHRISTMAS WITH MORRIS AND BORIS—Bernard Wiseman	(1–3)
THE CAT ON THE DOVREFELL—Tomie de Paola	(1–3)
THE CHRISTMAS KITTEN—Ruth and Latrobe Carroll	(1–3)
THE CHRISTMAS GIFT—Emily Arnold McCully	(1–3)

THE SILVER CHRISTMAS TREE—Pat Hutchins   (2–3)
THE CHRISTMAS GRUMP—Joseph Low   (2–3)
BENI'S FIRST CHANUKAH—Jane Zalben   (2–3)
HURRY HOME, GRANDMA!—Arielle North Olson   (2–3)
NUTTY'S CHRISTMAS—Claire Schumacher   (2–3)
PIGS AT CHRISTMAS—Arlene Dubanevich   (2–3)
BUNNIES AT CHRISTMAS TIME—Amy Ehrlich   (2–3)
ALL THOSE MOTHERS AT THE MANGER—Norma Farber   (2–3)
ROTTEN RALPH'S ROTTEN CHRISTMAS—Jack Gantos   (2–3)
HAPPY CHRISTMAS GEMMA—Sarah Hayes   (2–3)
A BAD START FOR SANTA—Sarah Hayes   (2–3)
BAH! HUMBUG?—Lorna Balian   (2–3)
LITTLE BEAR'S CHRISTMAS—Janice   (2–4)
CHRISTMAS PRESENT FROM A FRIEND—Yuriko Kimura   (2–4)
THE LEGEND OF OLD BEFANA—Tomie de Paola   (2–4)
THE CHRISTMAS EVE MYSTERY—Joan Lowery Nixon   (2–4)
HOW LITTLE PORCUPINE PLAYED CHRISTMAS—Joseph Slate   (2–4)
CHRISTMAS EVE—Edith Thacher Hurd   (2–4)
CHANUKKAH TREE—Eric Kimmel   (2–4)
MR. WILLOWLY'S CHRISTMAS TREE—Robert Barry   (2–4)
MADELINE'S CHRISTMAS—Ludwig Bemelmans   (2–4)
THE BERENSTAIN BEARS MEET SANTA BEAR—Stan and
  Jan Berenstain   (2–4)
THE BERENSTAIN BEARS' CHRISTMAS TREE—Stan and
  Jan Berenstain   (2–4)
THE DONKEY'S DREAM—Barbara Helen Berger   (2–4)
GEORGIE'S CHRISTMAS CAROL—Robert Bright   (2–4)
DECEMBER 24th—Denys Cazet   (2–4)
FAT SANTA—Margery Cuyler   (2–4)
THE CHRISTMAS WHALE—Roger Duvoisin   (2–4)
THE CHRISTMAS WOLF—Michel Gay   (2–4)
ANGELINA'S CHRISTMAS—Katharine Holabird   (2–4)
LUCY AND TOM'S CHRISTMAS—Shirley Hughes   (2–4)
MERRY CHRISTMAS, SPACE CASE—James Marshall   (2–4)
THE CHRISTMAS BOX—Eve Merriam   (2–4)
MOUSEKIN'S CHRISTMAS EVE—Edna Miller   (2–4)
THE NIGHT BEFORE CHRISTMAS—Clement C. Moore   (2–4)
ARTHUR'S CHRISTMAS—Marc Brown   (3–4)
I LOVE HANUKKAH—Myrilyn Hirsh   (3–4)
THE CHRISTMAS TRAIN—Ivan Gantschev   (3–4)
THE MOLE FAMILY'S CHRISTMAS—Russell Hoban   (3–4)
MRS. CLAUS'S CRAZY CHRISTMAS—Steven Kroll   (3–4)
SANTA'S CRASH-BANG CHRISTMAS—Steven Kroll   (3–4)
HOW THE GRINCH STOLE CHRISTMAS—Dr. Seuss   (3–4)
GUS WAS A CHRISTMAS GHOST—Jane Thayer   (3–4)

EFFECTIVE INSTRUCTION TIP OF THE MONTH

HOLD STUDENTS ACCOUNTABLE

Research in the area of teacher expectations tells us that many times we use techniques that unintentionally convey to some students that we don't expect them to answer questions and that they don't have to participate in the learning if they choose not to do so. Too many students, especially those in the low reading group, will choose not to answer if they can avoid it.

By using the techniques for distributing questions described earlier to make sure you are calling on all students regardless of whether or not they raise their hands, you are requiring more students to pay more attention, to stay engaged in the thinking process, and to learn. But, even using these techniques, a few students soon realize that they still don't have to bother paying attention or listening to the questions and thinking through answers because, if they get called on, they can simply indicate they don't know the answer and the teacher will quickly call on someone else.

To keep even the most determined non-listeners listening and actively learning, there are three more techniques to add to your repertoire for frequent use in your reading classes. These three techniques should be used when you ask a reading lesson question and a student can't or won't give an answer, or when a student gives an incorrect answer. The techniques are given below in the order in which you use them.

STEP 1. REPHRASE THE QUESTION—If you call on a student who does not know the question or gives an incorrect answer, rephrase the question in a simpler form. If the student still can't give the answer or gives an incorrect answer, move on to STEP 2.

STEP 2. PROVIDE CLUES AND HINTS—Your objective is to help the student come up with the right answer. This isn't a test time, so it's very much all right to help the student answer the question correctly. If the student still can't give the correct answer, quickly call on another student to give the answer.

STEP 3. COME BACK TO THE STUDENT AND HAVE HIM/HER REPEAT THE CORRECT ANSWER—This is an important step. If the student still cannot give the correct answer after STEP 2, you want to convey to that student that it is all right not to know the answer to a question when you are called on but you must listen to the answer when someone else gives it and you must give that answer when the teacher calls on you in a moment. Therefore, after another student gives the correct answer, state that the answer is correct, then repeat the question and call on the student who was unable to answer the question and have him/her repeat the answer that was just given.

SANTA CLAUS GAME
(Grades 2–6)

PURPOSE: Multi-purpose: word recognition, synonyms, antonyms, definitions, prefixes, suffixes, rhyming words, vowel sounds, consonant blends

MATERIALS: —16″ × 20″ piece of white posterboard
  —Santa Claus gameboard
  —Santa Claus Color Me Game Sheet
  —black fine-line marker
  —permanent felt-tip markers (assorted colors)
  —paper cutter
  —oaktag or unlined file cards
  —laminating materials
  —duplicator paper
  —photocopier or duplicator machine
  —4 game markers
  —2 dice
  —1 box of crayons

PREPARATION: Using an opaque projector, reproduce the gameboard onto a 16″ × 20″ piece of white posterboard with a permanent, black felt-tip marker. The game pathway should be made up of 2″ × 2″ squares, eight squares along the bottom and the top of the gameboard, ten squares on the left and the right sides of the gameboard.

Next, determine the skill to be reinforced with the game. Cut 2″ × 3″ cards from oaktag or unlined file cards. Select the actual words (or phonics or word attack items) to be incorporated into the game. Write a different word (or phonics or word attack) item on each card. Laminate the gameboard and the cards.

Using a photocopy machine or duplicator machine, reproduce the Santa Claus Color Me Game Sheet onto white duplicator paper. Each player will need a Color Me Game Sheet each time the game is played. You will also need four game markers, a pair of dice, and a box of crayons.

GAME DIRECTIONS: This game is played by two to four players. The cards are shuffled and placed face down beside the gameboard. Each player must have a Color Me Game Sheet. The box of crayons should be placed nearby. The game markers are placed on the START block.

The first player throws the dice, moves the marker forward the indicated number of spaces, draws the card and performs the task (i.e., pronounces the word, gives a synonym or antonym of the word, gives a definition, names a word containing the vowel sound indicated, names a word with the indicated prefix or suffix, depending on how the game is set up by the teacher). Upon successful completion of the task, the player gets to color in the item on his or her Color Me Game Sheet that is found on the space on which he or she landed on the gameboard. It is then the next player's turn to throw the dice, etc. If a player can not correctly perform the task on the card, no item is colored in on the Color Me Game Sheet. The game continues in this manner until a player has completely colored in the Santa Claus picture on his or her Color Me Game Sheet. In order to land on all of the spaces required to completely color in the Color Me Game Sheet, it will be necessary for the players to go around the gameboard a number of times. It will also be necessary to reshuffle the task cards and place them in a pile face down each time the players have gone through the entire stack of cards. If a player lands on a space that has already been colored on the player's Color Me Game sheet, the player simply draws the card and performs the task but omits coloring the already colored item on the Color Me Game Sheet. The WINNER is the first player with a completely colored Color Me Game Sheet.

START

Santa Claus Game

Santa Claus Game

WREATH FLASH CARDS

(Grades 1–6)

PURPOSE: To develop recognition of new vocabulary words in the reading lesson

MATERIALS: —heavy white art paper or white tagboard
—green-watercolor felt-tip marker
—red-watercolor felt-tip marker
—black fine-line marker
—Wreath Flash Card patterns
—photocopier or duplicator machine
—laminating materials
—black transparency pen or black dry-mark pen

PREPARATION: Duplicate or photocopy the wreath card patterns onto heavy white art paper or onto white tagboard. Using a water-color green felt-tip marker, color the wreath. Color the berries and bow red with a red-watercolor felt-tip marker. Use the black fine-line marker to outline the bow, berries, and wreath. Then laminate and cut out each of the wreath flash cards.

PROCEDURE: Using a black dry-mark pen or a transparency pen, print a different vocabulary word from the reading lesson in the center of each wreath flash card.

Now you are ready to use the cards to introduce and drill on the new vocabulary words in the reading lesson. First, introduce the new vocabulary words in the manner indicated in the teacher's manual for the basal reading program you are using. Then use the wreath flash cards as fun flash cards to reinforce recognition of those new words.

When the instructional activity is completed, wipe off the words and write new words for the next reading group or for the next lesson.

Samples

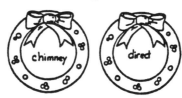

WREATH FLASH CARD PATTERN PAGE

SYNONYM SANTAS

(Grades 3–6)

PURPOSE: Vocabulary development and reinforcement

MATERIALS: —white tagboard or white coverstock
—black Flair pen
—red-watercolor felt-tip marker
—turquoise-blue colored pencil
—Synonym Santas patterns
—photocopier or duplicator machine
—laminating materials
—scissors
—black dry-mark pen or black transparency pen
—box
—attractive contact paper
—permanent, black felt-tip pen

PREPARATION: Photocopy or duplicate the Synonym Santas pattern page onto white coverstock or white tagboard (available at any office supply company) to make 16–20 Santas. Use a red-watercolor felt-tip marker to color the hats on each of the Santas. Color the eyes on the Santas blue with a turquoise-blue colored pencil. Then use a black Flair pen to outline all of the lines on each of the Santas. Cut out each Santa.

Next, select 16–20 vocabulary words that have synonyms. The words should be appropriate for the reading level of the students. They can be selected from past lessons in your reading book or from the list of synonyms provided at the end of this book. On each Santa print a different vocabulary word on the white, furry border of the hat. (See the illustration.) Laminate the Santas and cut them from the laminating film. Then place the Santas in a box covered with attractive contact paper and print the activity title, SYN-ONYM SANTAS, on the top of the box with a permanent, black felt-tip marker.

PROCEDURE: Students do this activity independently. Using a black dry-mark pen or a black transparency pen, have students write on the beard of each Santa the synonym of the word on the hat of the Santa. If a student cannot recall a synonym for the word on a hat, the student can look the word up in a dictionary to find a synonym. When a student has completed the activity, check the student's work, then have the student wipe off his or her answers. The activity is then ready for the next student.

NOTE: This activity can be made self-correcting. Simply write the synonym or synonyms on the back of each Santa. When a student completes the activity, he or she can check the answers by simply turning the Santas over and comparing the answers.

SYNONYM SANTAS PATTERN PAGE

VOCABULARY CHAINS

(Grades 3–6)

PURPOSE: Vocabulary/word meaning

MATERIALS: —assorted colors of construction paper
  —paper cutter
  —white school glue or stapler and staples
  —black, fine-line felt-tip marking pen

PREPARATION: Cut a large number of 1″ × 5″ strips of various colors of construction paper. Set the strips of construction paper on a work table along with a bottle of white school glue, a stapler, a black, fine-line felt-tip marking pen and a dictionary.

PROCEDURE: Students are going to make long paper chains with new vocabulary words and their meanings. Have students look for new vocabulary words in their reading. The words might be from their reading books, library books, newspapers, etc. When a student finds a new vocabulary word, he/she should go to the work table, select a construction paper strip, neatly print the vocabulary word in the center of the strip, and loop the strip through the previous loop of the vocabulary paper chain with the word side facing out. The student then can either glue or staple the paper loop to form another link in the chain. Next, the student should print a synonym or short definition on the inside of the loop, facing the same direction as the vocabulary word. A dictionary can be used to determine the meaning of the word.

125

When the chain gets really long, have students start a new chain. The completed chains can be used to decorate a class Christmas tree or they can simply be strung along the top of the chalkboard or along a window sill in attractive draping loops.

Students will enjoy searching for new vocabulary words so that they can add words to the chain. This is a good activity to do over a several-week period of time as students will enjoy making the chains grow longer and longer and longer.

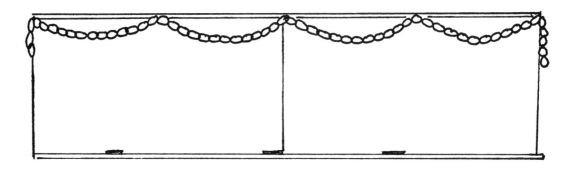

BONUS IDEA OF THE MONTH

MAGIC HAT REVIEW TECHNIQUE
(Grades 1–6)

Just as Frosty the Snowman's magic hat made him come alive, using the Magic Hat Review Technique in your classroom can make review and practice of new vocabulary words come alive for your students. Use of the technique can also magically "soak up" some of the wasted minutes in your classroom, turning them into valuable learning time. All you will need is a man's hat, stacks of several colors of unlined file cards, and a felt-tip marker. The number of different colors of file cards needed will be equal to the number of reading groups in your classroom.

After new vocabulary words have been introduced to a reading group, print them on one color of unlined file cards. Put the cards in the hat. Over a period of days and weeks, continue adding new word cards as new vocabulary words are introduced to the group. The vocabulary words for one reading group should always be printed on the same color cards. Use a similar procedure for words introduced to your other reading groups. But, be sure to print each group's words on different-colored cards.

Whenever you have a couple of minutes of unexpected wait time during the day, simply reach for the magic hat, shuffle the cards around in the hat, draw a card out, show it to the whole class, then, noting the color, call on someone from the appropriate reading group to read the word or read the word and tell its meaning. Students in the primary grades will probably be asked to simply identify the word, thus working on word recognition. Students in the intermediate grades will probably be asked to identify the word and tell its meaning, synonym, or antonym, thus working on word recognition and word meaning.

After a student reads the word (and tells its meaning at the intermediate levels), put the word back in the magic hat, shuffle the cards around and draw out another. Continue in this manner. Be sure to keep the activity moving along quickly. Ham it up a bit as you draw out the words. The students will love it!

Sometimes you may wish to vary the activity a bit to use the word cards to reinforce phonics or word attack skills. After a student identifies the word, you may ask the student to indicate the vowel sound, the consonant blend, the number of syllables, the prefix, or the suffix found in the word. The possibilities are many.

This activity is perfect for use when the class unexpectedly has a couple of minutes of waiting time without anything to do. This may be while you wait for the art or music teacher to arrive in your room, while you wait for the arrival of students on a late bus, while you wait for a messenger to tell you it is time for your class to go to an assembly, etc. You will find a number of opportunities to use it during the school day each week. Keep adding new words to the magic hat and you can use it week after week, month after month.

SANTA'S SACK TACHIST-O-SCOPE

(Grades 1–4)

PURPOSE: Know synonyms
   (*Variations*: recognize sight words, letters, letter-sound relationships, compound words, antonyms, etc.)

MATERIALS: —white railroad board or posterboard
   —Santa's Sack Tachist-o-Scope
   —white tagboard of heavy white art paper
   —pencil
   —black fine-line marker
   —permanent felt-tip markers—assorted colors
   —colored pencils—assorted colors
   —scissors
   —tracing paper
   —carbon paper
   —laminating materials
   —art knife
   —washable transparency pen or dry-mark pen

PREPARATION: Trace the Santa's Sack Tachist-o-Scope pattern onto a sheet of tracing paper. Place the tracing paper on top of a sheet of carbon paper. Place these on top of a piece of white railroad board or posterboard. Trace over the tracing to transfer the Santa's sack drawing on the tracing paper to the railroad board. Remove the tracing paper and carbon paper. Use a black fine-line pen and/or black felt-tip pen to outline the drawing. Color the toy sack with colored pencils or felt-tip markers in an attractive manner. Cut out the toy sack and laminate. Trim the laminating film from the cut-out. Using the art knife, cut two horizontal slots, approximately 2″ long and 1″ apart, on the toy sack. Cut the tagboard or art paper into 2″ × 11″ strips and laminate.

PROCEDURE: Select the words for practice in the reading group. Using a washable transparency pen or dry-mark pen, print the words on the laminated strip, one beneath the other and approximately 1″ apart. Put the word strip behind the Santa's Sack Tachist-o-Scope and thread it through the bottom slot, then back through the top slot.

To use, slide the word strip up exposing a word. Call on a student to read the word aloud and say a synonym of the word. Then pull the word strip up to expose the next word and call on another student to read the word and give its synonym. Continue in this manner.

When finished with the vocabulary practice on the Santa's Sack Tachist-o-Scope, simply remove the word strip and wipe off the words with a damp paper towel. New words can be written on the word strip and the Santa's Sack Tachist-o-Scope is ready to use with another reading group.

SANTA'S SACK TACHIST-O-SCOPE

Motivation Book Report Forms

A GOOD SPORTS BOOK! and SPORTS! SPORTS! SPORTS!
(Grades 3–6)

Set up a display table of good sports books appropriate for your grade level. These should include fiction, non-fiction, and how-to-do-it, sports-related books. Your school librarian or the children's librarian at your local public library can assist you in finding good sports books for your display. Duplicate copies of the Motivation Book Report Forms, A GOOD SPORTS BOOK! and SPORTS! SPORTS! SPORTS!. Place copies of each of the forms on the book display table.

Ask students to select a sports-related book to read. The book can be selected from the display table or from the library. Hold up a couple of sports books with which you are familiar and talk enthusiastically about them. Encourage some of the students to tell about some good sports books they have read in the past. Then point out to the students the two book report forms you have placed on the book display table. Explain that after they have finished reading a sports-related book, they are to write a book report on one of these two book report forms. After completing a book report form, students may wish to lightly color the ball on the form.

Name _____ **Date** _____

A GOOD SPORTS BOOK!

Title of book _____

Author _____

_____ Fiction   _____ Nonfiction   _____ How-to-Do-It

This book was written about the sport of _____

Tell about the book. _____

_____

_____

_____

_____

Was this a book others in the class would like to read?

_____

Why? _____

_____

Name —————

Date —————

SPORTS! SPORTS! SPORTS!

Title of book —————

Author —————

The book was written about the sport of —————

The book was ——— Fiction ——— Nonfiction

Tell about the book. —————
—————
—————
—————

Who else in your class would enjoy reading this book?
—————
—————

VOCABULARY PRACTICE TRANSPARENCY

Use this page to make a transparency for developing word recognition or for vocabulary/word meaning practice. Write the **words to be practiced** on the ornaments with a washable transparency pen.

VOCABULARY PRACTICE TRANSPARENCY

Use this page to make a transparency for developing word recognition or for vocabulary/word meaning practice. **Write the words to be practiced** on the presents with a washable transparency pen.

Name ———————————————— **Date** ————————————————

DESCRIBE THAT CHARACTER

Title of story ————————————————————————————

————————————————————————————————

Author ————————————————————————————————

List each of the characters in the story. Beside each character name, write three adjectives that describe that character.

————————————————————————————————

————————————————————————————————

————————————————————————————————

————————————————————————————————

————————————————————————————————

————————————————————————————————

————————————————————————————————

————————————————————————————————

————————————————————————————————

————————————————————————————————

————————————————————————————————

————————————————————————————————

————————————————————————————————

————————————————————————————————

Name your favorite character: ————————————————————

Story Extension Activity

Name _____

Date _____

EXPAND YOUR VOCABULARY

Title of story _____

Author _____

Briefly tell about the story.
_____
_____

List 5 new words you found in the story.

1. _____ 2. _____
3. _____ 4. _____
5. _____

Look up the dictionary meanings of 3 of those words.
Write the 3 words and their meanings below.

1. _____
2. _____
3. _____

In the story, find 6 interesting words that tell how
something looked.

1. _____ 2. _____
3. _____ 4. _____
5. _____ 6. _____

Find 2 phrases that describe how something looked.

1. _____
2. _____

Find 2 words or phrases that describe how something
sounded, smelled, or felt.

1. _____
2. _____

Reading Motivation Bulletin Board

BOOKS . . . PERFECT TO GIVE AND TO RECEIVE
(Grades 1–6)

PURPOSE: Reading motivation

MATERIALS: —white bulletin board paper
—bulletin board pattern
—permanent felt-tip markers (assorted colors)
—crayons
—stapler and staples
—opaque projector or overhead projector and transparency
—holiday wrapping paper (optional)

PREPARATION: Cover a bulletin board with white bulletin board paper. Use an opaque projector to project the bulletin board picture on the next page onto the bulletin board. Trace the title lettering and the picture onto the bulletin board with various appropriate colors of felt-tip markers. Then color the picture with the felt-tip markers and/or crayons. (*Optional*: You may wish to use cut-out pieces of real wrapping paper stapled to the bulletin board picture to represent several of the already wrapped books.)

NOTE: If an opaque projector is not available, make a transparency of the bulletin board. Then, using an overhead projector, project the illustration onto the bulletin board paper for tracing.

JANUARY

EFFECTIVE INSTRUCTION TIP OF THE MONTH

THE READING/WRITING CONNECTION

In the past we taught reading every day and we had an occasional creative writing assignment. However, recent expansion of our understanding of how children learn to read shows the importance of emphasizing writing along with reading. Students from first grade right on up through sixth grade and higher need daily opportunities to write. The writing we are talking about is not handwriting practice in handwriting books, nor is it writing to fill in the blanks in workbooks or on worksheets, although these too are important for other reasons. The writing we are talking about involves students writing stories, writing about their experiences, and writing about whatever interests them.

To maximize growth in reading skill development, students should have daily writing opportunities. Writing and reading go hand in hand. They reinforce the same skills. Each one helps to increase understanding of the other one in a natural way. They work together.

This means that we need to consistently incorporate writing into our lesson plans. To find time for students to write more, it may be necessary to take a hard look at some of the reading seatwork activities you are having your students do. Some of the workbook pages and duplicator pages that go with the reading program are very necessary for skill development and reinforcement. However, some of these pages are unnecessary. They work on skills that students have already thoroughly mastered. If you look at each of the workbook pages and duplicator pages you would normally assign and decide to eliminate the ones that are unneeded, you could free up some additional time during the school year for writing activities. Beyond that, there is usually a fair amount of wasted time during seatwork activities. Students finish the workbook pages and other seatwork quickly and then find nonconstructive ways to spend time. This otherwise wasted time could be turned into writing time.

Sometimes you may wish to give students a story starter. If you do this, be sure to lead the students in a brainstorming session in which they generate lots of ideas about the topic before you have them start to write. This will result in all students loaded with ideas as they begin to write. Sometimes you may wish to have students write a new ending for a story they have just read in the reading book. Or, perhaps they might write a letter to a character in the story explaining what he/she might have done differently. Or, perhaps they could simply write about what they liked best about the story. The writing possibilities that can be created based on a reading textbook story are endless!

Other times you may wish to let students write about whatever interests them. Sometimes younger children like drawing a picture then writing a story about that picture. For first grade students that story may only be one or two sentences long. Having students draw a picture first before writing allows them time to generate lots of ideas about what they want to write. Then when they are ready to begin writing, they are really ready!

As you begin incorporating writing into your reading program, you will want to read a couple of good books on how to teach writing. Our understanding of how to teach writing has changed dramatically in the last couple of years. If you are not familiar with the developmental stages in children's writing and the writing process, you should set this as a priority.

Deciding to incorporate writing into the reading program is a major step toward improving the reading skill development of your students. Make it a New Year's resolution and begin today.

Multi-Purpose Gameboard

THE HAPPY SNOWMAN
(Grades 1–6)

PURPOSE: Multi-purpose gameboard: vowel sounds, consonants, consonant blends and digraphs, prefixes, suffixes, synonyms, antonyms, homonyms, rhyming words, sight word recognition

MATERIALS: —18″ × 18″ piece of light blue railroad board or posterboard
—The Happy Snowman gameboard
—9″ × 14″ piece of heavy white art paper
—rubber cement
—permanent felt-tip markers—assorted colors
—black fine-line marker
—yardstick
—scissors
—cellophane tape or masking tape
—liquid white tempera paint
—old toothbrush
—small piece of screen
—old newspaper
—game pieces
—die

PREPARATION: On a sheet of blue railroad board or posterboard, draw the pathway of the gameboard using a black felt-tip pen. Tape the piece of heavy white art paper to the chalkboard. Using an opaque projector, project the gameboard illustration of the snowman onto the art paper and trace the illustration. Remove the illustration from the chalkboard. Outline the snowman with black felt-tip pen. Color the snowman's broom, hat, etc. attractively. Cut out the snowman and glue it onto the gameboard with rubber cement. Print the game name on the gameboard.

Carefully cover the gameboard pathway with old newspaper. Then spatter-paint the gameboard picture area with white tempera paint. To do this, dip the bristles of an old toothbrush into the tempera paint and rub the toothbrush back and forth over a small piece of screen. This will result in white paint splatters over the picture creating the effect of snow. Let the gameboard dry overnight, then laminate.

Next, decide upon the skill you wish to reinforce on the gameboard. With a permanent, black felt-tip marker, print different words or letters on each block of the gameboard pathway, depending on the skill the game is to reinforce.

You will also need three or four markers and a die.

NOTE: To change the words or letters on the laminated gameboard pathway, simply spray with hair spray and wipe off the words/letters with a tissue. The gameboard pathway will be erased and ready for new words or letters to be printed along the pathway with a permanent felt-tip marker.

PROCEDURE: This game can be played by two to four players. Students place their markers on *START*. The first player throws the die and moves forward the indicated number of spaces and performs the task (i.e., pronounces the word and gives its synonym or antonym, names the vowel and says a word that contains that vowel, etc.) for the space on which he/she landed. If the player cannot perform the task, his/her marker must be moved back one space. If the player lands on one of the corner blocks, he/she must follow the instructions on that block. It is then the next player's turn to throw the die, etc. The WINNER is the first player to land on *FINISH*.

Very Cold Weather Take 1 extra

Heat Wave Snowman melting move Back 3 Spaces

The Happy Snowman

Finish

Start

Beautiful Blizzard move forward 2 spaces

TELEVISION FLASH CARDS

(Grades 1–6)

PURPOSE: To develop word recognition of new vocabulary words in the reading lesson

MATERIALS: —heavy white art paper or white tagboard
—brown watercolor felt-tip marker
—black Flair pen (or other fine-line marker)
—Television Flash Card patterns
—duplicator machine
—laminating materials
—black transparency pen or dry-mark pen
—scissors

PREPARATION: Duplicate the television card patterns onto white tagboard or onto heavy white art paper. Color the television, except the screen, brown. Leave the television screen white. Use the black Flair pen to outline all of the lines and details on the televisions. Then laminate and cut out each of the television flash cards.

PROCEDURE: Using a black dry-mark pen or a black transparency pen, print a different vocabulary word from the reading lesson in the center of each television flash card.

Now you are ready to use the cards to introduce and drill on the new vocabulary words in the reading lesson. First, introduce the new vocabulary in the manner indicated in the teacher's manual for the basal reading program you are using. Then use the television flash cards as fun flash cards to reinforce recognition of those new words. After the teacher-directed reading lesson is over, you may wish to place the flash cards in an accessible location where pairs of students can pick them up and practice them together.

The Television Flash Cards can be used over and over for new lessons or new reading groups. Simply wipe off the words and print on new words.

TELEVISION FLASH CARD PATTERN PAGE

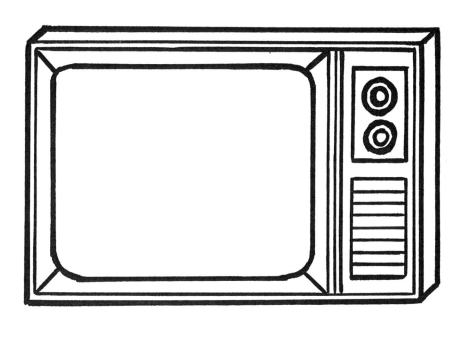

ANTONYM SLEDS

(Grades 2–6)

PURPOSE: Vocabulary development

MATERIALS: —light tan construction paper

—Flair pens (black, red, and yellow)

—red watercolor felt-tip marker

—Antonym Sleds patterns

—duplicator machine

—laminating materials

—scissors

—black dry-mark pen or black transparency pen

—box

—attractive self-stick vinyl

—permanent, black felt-tip marker

PREPARATION: Duplicate the Antonym Sled pattern page onto light tan construction paper to make 12–24 sleds. Use a red-watercolor felt-tip marker to color the steering bar on each of the sleds. Use a yellow Flair pen to color the metal runners. Then use a black Flair pen to outline all lines on each of the sleds.

Next, select 12–24 vocabulary words that have antonyms. The words should be appropriate for the reading level of the students. They can be selected from past lessons in the reading book or from the list of antonyms provided at the end of this book. Using a red Flair pen, print a different vocabulary word on each sled. Cut out each sled. Laminate the sleds and cut them from the laminating film. Then place the sleds in a box covered with attractive self-stick vinyl and print the activity title ANTONYM SLEDS on the top of the box with a permanent, black felt-tip marker.

PROCEDURE: Students can do this activity independently. Using a black dry-mark pen or black transparency pen, have students write on each sled an antonym of the word on the sled. If a student cannot recall an antonym for the word on a sled, the student can look the word up in the dictionary to find its meaning, and then think of an antonym. Or, the student can look the word up in a beginning thesaurus and select an antonym of the word. When a student has completed the activity, check the student's work, then have the student wipe off the answers. The activity is then ready for the next student.

NOTE: This activity can be made self-correcting. Simply write the antonym or antonyms on the back of each sled. Then, when a student completes the activity, he or she can check the answers by simply turning the sleds over and comparing the answers.

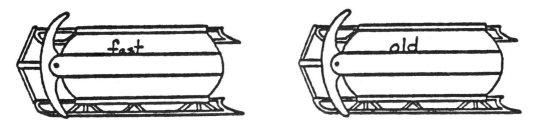

Primary Level Examples

Intermediate Level Example

ANTONYM SLED PATTERN PAGE

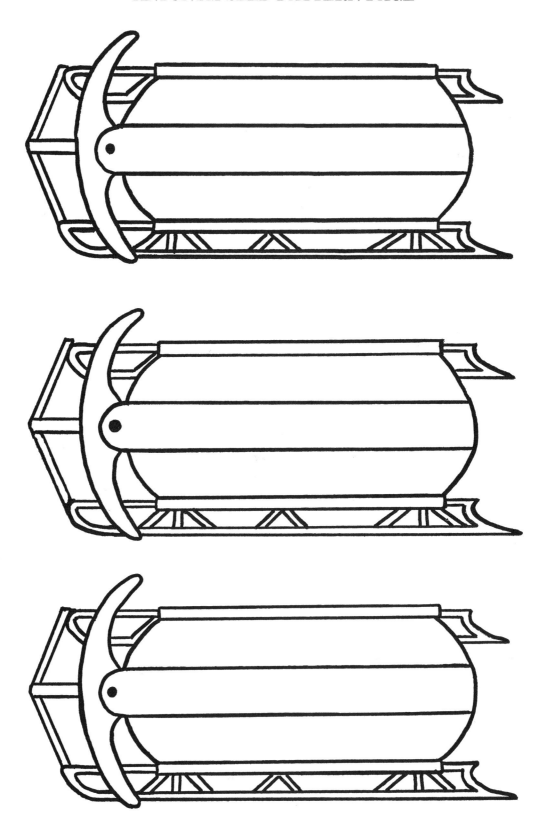

SYNONYM CHECKERS

(Grades 3–6)

PURPOSE: Vocabulary development: synonyms
    (*Variation*: vocabulary development: antonyms)

MATERIALS: —14″ × 14″ piece of colored railroad board or posterboard
           —pencil
           —black felt-tip pen
           —black fine-line marking pen
           —yardstick
           —laminating materials
           —1 set of checkers

PREPARATION: Using a yardstick and a pencil, draw the checkerboard squares onto a 14″ × 14″ piece of colored railroad board or posterboard. The checker squares should be 1½″ × 1½″. The gameboard border should be 1″ wide. Therefore, you will mark off 1″, then eight 1½″ intervals. This will form the borders and the eight 1½″ squares each direction. With the black felt-tip pen, color in every other square, checkerboard style. Next, select vocabulary words that have synonyms from the reading book or select appropriate level synonyms from the synonym lists provided at the end of this book. Write one word of the synonym pair on each non-black gameboard square (see the gameboard illustration). Laminate the gameboard.

    You will also need a set of checkers. These can be taken from a regular checker game or they can be purchased separately, very inexpensively, at most toy stores.

PROCEDURE: Students play this game like regular checkers, except when a checker is moved on a square, the player must say the word on the square and give a synonym. If a player jumps a checker, he/she must say the word and give the synonym for the word found on the square of the checker jumped as well as the one landed upon.

NOTE: *Instead of writing the vocabulary words on the gameboard before laminating, you may wish to laminate the gameboard first, without the words. Then write the words on the gameboard with a fine-line, permanent felt-tip marker. When students have played the game a number of times and are familiar with the words, you can then erase the vocabulary words and write new words on the gameboard. Simply spray the words on the laminated surface with hair spray and wipe off the words with a tissue. The words will be erased and the checkerboard will be ready for new words to be written on the laminated surface with a permanent felt-tip marker.*

PENGUINS AND ICEBERGS

(Grades 1–6)

PURPOSE: Multi-purpose match-up activity.
(Examples: Matching capital and lower case letters, vowel sounds, synonyms, antonyms, homonyms, rhyming words, contractions, or words to definitions)

MATERIALS: —heavy white paper, cover stock, or large index cards
—Penguin and Iceberg patterns
—black fine-line marker
—red, permanent, thin-line felt tip pen
—scissors
—laminating materials

PREPARATION: Using the patterns, reproduce penguins and icebergs in quantity needed. Laminate and cut out each piece. Using a red, thin-line, permanent felt-tip pen, write letters or words on the penguins and the corresponding letters or words on the icebergs.

NOTE: This activity can be made self-correcting by writing a different numeral on the reverse side of each penguin and the same numeral on the reverse side of the iceberg that matches the penguin. When a child has completed the activity, the penguins and icebergs can be turned over to see if the numerals on the reverse side of the matched penguins and icebergs are identical.

PROCEDURE: Have students match penguins to corresponding icebergs.

PENGUIN AND ICEBERG PATTERN PAGE

CREATE WORDSEARCH PUZZLES

(Grades 3–6)

Children love to find the words in wordsearch puzzles. But many times the wordsearch puzzles available from the various publishers are simply fun time-fillers. They have very little learning value because the words found in the puzzle do not relate in any way to classroom instruction. Beyond that, many times the words in the puzzles are words with which the students are already very familiar and to which the students do not need additional exposure. Other times, some of the words in the puzzles may be so hard that the students don't even recognize them and don't know the meaning of them. The use of word puzzles that completely miss the instructional needs of students can many times be a misuse of valuable learning time.

PURPOSE: Word recognition
MATERIALS: —wordsearch puzzle grid
　　　　　　—typewriter or fine-line felt-tip marker
PREPARATION: Photocopy of blank wordsearch puzzle grid. On a piece of scratch paper, begin making a list of words you wish to use in the wordsearch puzzle. Often you will wish to select vocabulary words from recent stories in the reading book. Sometimes you may wish to select words relating to a holiday or perhaps words needing review from a chapter just completed in the science or social studies book. The number of words you will plan to incorporate into your wordsearch puzzle will vary with the grade level of your students. Be careful not to include so many words that the puzzle will become unpleasant drudgery for the students.

Once you have selected the words you wish to use in the puzzle, you need to print them on the photocopy of the wordsearch puzzle grid. The words should be printed horizontally with the letters going from left to right or vertically with the letters of the word descending. At the fifth or sixth grade level you may also wish to fill in some of the words diagonally with the letters going from upper left to lower right.

NOTE: At no time should you spell the words backwards from right to left or from the bottom up. Asking students to find words that are printed backwards is educationally unsound and a waste of learning time! For transfer of learning to take place, the activity must present the words in a manner students will find them in real reading situations.

After you have written in the words on the puzzle grid, fill in the remaining blocks with miscellaneous letters. Next, below the wordsearch puzzle, list the words you have incorporated into the puzzle.

Duplicate or photocopy the puzzle in the quantity needed for the students in the group.

PROCEDURE: Distribute copies of the wordsearch puzzle. Tell the students they are to find and circle in the puzzle each of the words listed below the puzzle. Tell them to cross out each word below the puzzle after they find the word in the puzzle.

WORDSEARCH PUZZLE

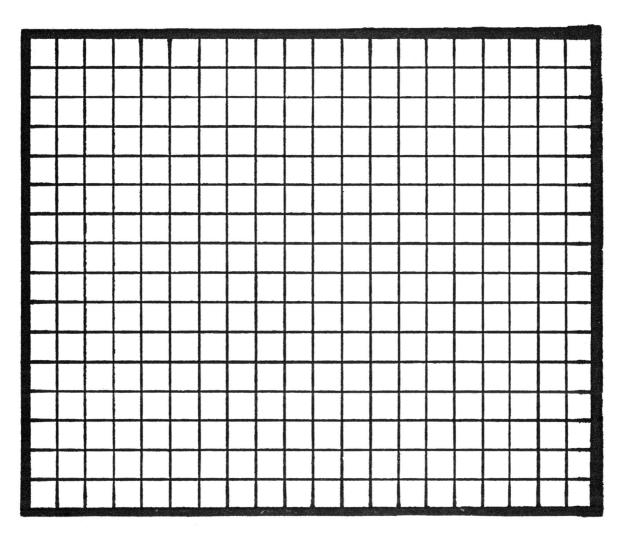

BONUS IDEA OF THE MONTH

QUICK AND EASY BOOK COVERS

Here is a quick and very easy way to make attractive book covers for stories your students write. More than that, while these book covers are only stapled together, the staples won't pull out through hundreds of openings and closings of the book!

MATERIALS: —discontinued wallpaper sample book
            —stapler and staples
            —art knife or scissors
            —paper cutter
            —permanent felt-tip markers, assorted colors

PREPARATION: Obtain a discontinued wallpaper sample book from a wallpaper store. Many wallpaper stores give these away free to teachers. Some sell them for one or two dollars a book. Wallpaper sample books come in different sizes. You will want to get a large one with vinyl wallpaper samples.

PROCEDURE: After students have finished the final copy of their stories, you can quickly make bookcovers for their stories. Simply cut out attractive sheets of wallpaper from the sample book. The easiest way to do this is to slice them out by running an art knife down each page you wish to remove. If you don't have an art knife, use a pair of scissors and cut them out. Next, fold a sheet of wallpaper in half and crease (see illustration #1). Place the pages of a student's story on top of the folded wallpaper with the left side of the pages lined up against the fold. Next, you will need to trim some of the excess wallpaper away to make it more manageable to work with. Using a paper cutter, trim the top and bottom of the wallpaper bookcover so that only about 1½″ of extra wallpaper remains at both the top and bottom. Then trim the right edge so that about 3 extra inches remain. Do not trim the left side where the fold is.

Next, place the story pages inside the book cover, with the left side of the story pages right up against the book cover fold. Close the book cover and staple the pages to the book cover along the fold side and in about ¼″ from the fold. Two staples are all that will be needed. Next, fold the top book cover back and crease about ½″ from the first fold (see illustration #2). Then fold the top book cover back to cover the book again. This fold and crease should line up exactly with the very first book cover fold (see illustration #3). Now turn the book over and fold this side with the same two-step folding procedure (see illustrations #4 and #5). Turn the book over, front side up, folds still in place, and staple three staples along the left side about ⅓″ in from the crease. Use a paper cutter to trim the excess wallpaper from the top, bottom, and right side of the book. The final step is to print the book title on the book cover with a permanent felt-tip marker.

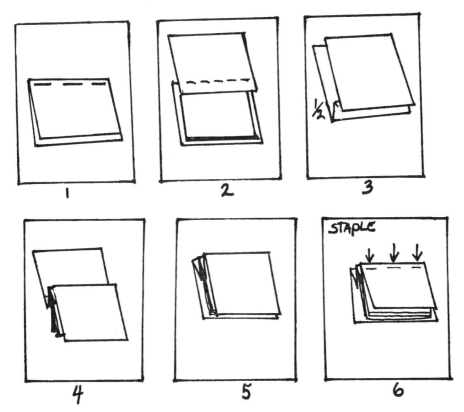

The book is now nicely covered with an attractive vinyl cover. The extra folding and stapling steps create a cover that will not pull out at the staples. The whole procedure takes less than two minutes from start to finish. It is such a quick process, you can cover a number of students' books in a short time. Furthermore, the process is so easy that students third grade and up can be taught to bind their own books.

With this technique, you can often make books out of your students' stories. These books can be displayed on a table or added to your classroom bookcase so that students can read and enjoy each others stories.

STUDY BUDDIES

(Grades 1–6)

There are a number of students in every class who will slop down answers on reading worksheets and workbook pages without really reading the material thoroughly and without taking the time to carefully figure out the correct answers. They simply want to get the worksheets done as fast as they can so that they can get on to other things. You can tell these students to take their time, to read each item carefully, and to check over their answers when they are finished, but your statements fall on deaf ears. These students time and again turn in papers with numerous errors.

To counteract hurriedly slopped out papers by students who aren't half trying, try having students work in pairs to complete assigned worksheets and workbook pages. When they work in pairs, you will find students will really read the material carefully, discuss the answer possibilities, explain answers to each other, and *work* on the assignment. The difference in quality of thinking and quality of effort will amaze you!

SICK KITS

(Grades 1–4)

The cold and flu season has arrived. Why not prepare several "Sick Kits" containing various reading-oriented items to help keep children who are sick at home occupied in fun but beneficial ways?

First you will need to get a couple of small, inexpensive overnight bags. You may be able to find a couple of these really cheap at garage sales. In each overnight bag, place a number of items to help sick children pass the time. Some items may be appropriate at some grade levels and not others. Some possibilities include:

—books
—a couple of *high motivation* reading worksheets
—a read-along book with accompanying tape or record
—a reading game
—some stationery and a pen with colored ink

Use your creative-thinking ability to come up with additional things to include. You may also want to purchase a number of get-well cards.

When a student is going to be out sick a number of days, parents can call you and request the loan of a Sick Kit. Before sending the Sick Kit home, you may wish to add a get-well card addressed to the sick child and signed by all of the other students and yourself.

When the child returns to school, he or she is responsible for bringing back the Sick Kit. Your students and their parents will love it!

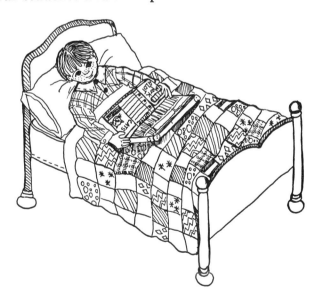

b and d CONFUSION CORRECTION TECHNIQUE
(Grades 1–2)

Many students in first and second grade have difficulty determining which letter is a *b* and which is a *d*. At these grade levels the confusion is usually caused by a simple lack of experience with the alphabet. For a few children it is caused by a visual perception problem with resulting reversal problems. Difficulty in determining which letter is a *b* and which letter is a *d* can cause problems for a child in sight word recognition, in sounding out unknown words, in spelling, and in writing.

To help children overcome this problem, here is a terrific technique you can teach your students. Have the students make fists with both hands, with hands in front of them, palms facing toward chest, and both thumbs up toward the ceiling. In this position, the left hand forms a *b* and the right hand forms a *d*.

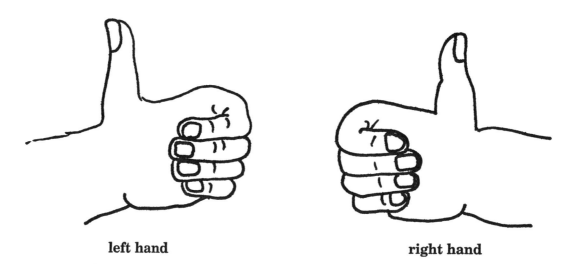

left hand   right hand

With hands in this position, have students begin to say the alphabet, "a . . . b . . ." When they come to the letter *b*, remind them that *b* comes before *d* in the alphabet. Have them look at their hands and point out that when they are reading a page, they start on the left side and read to the right. Therefore, what is on the left side comes before what is on the right. Show them that their left hand is forming the letter *b* and the letter *d* made by the right hand comes after the letter *b* made by the left hand as they "read" the letters formed by their hands, just as the letter *d* comes after the letter *b* in the alphabet.

Next, explain that when they come to a word with a *b* or a *d* and they can't remember which letter is which, all they have to do is put their hands in this position with their thumbs up, and softly begin to say the alphabet to themselves as they look at their hands as though they were reading across a page. Doing this, *b* comes before *d*, therefore the left hand is showing the *b* and the right hand is the *d*. Then all they have to do is compare the letter in the word with the *b* and *d* formed by their hands to determine which is which.

If a child is trying to spell a word that begins with a *b* or a *d*, but can't remember which letter goes in which direction, all the child needs to do is put his or her hands into the *b-d* positions, think *b* comes before *d* in the alphabet, and note the shapes of the letters formed by his or her hands. The child can then determine how to form the needed letter.

First and second grade students will catch on to this technique very quickly and apply it often. Off and on through the day you will spot students using the technique when they are trying to figure out a word in their reading and when they are writing, trying to spell a word with a *b* or a *d*. When students no longer need this "crutch" they will automatically stop using it.

SNOWMAN TACHIST-O-SCOPE

(Grades 1–4)

PURPOSE: To name rhyming words

(*Variations*: sight word practice, letter recognition, letter-sound relation-ships, compound words)

MATERIALS: —white railroad board or posterboard
—Snowman Tachist-o-Scope
—white tagboard or heavy art paper
—pencil
—colored pencils (assorted colors)
—felt-tip markers (assorted colors)
—scissors
—tracing paper
—carbon paper
—laminating materials
—art knife
—washable transparency pen or dry-mark pen

PREPARATION: Trace the Snowman Tachist-o-Scope pattern onto a sheet of tracing paper. Place the tracing paper on top of a sheet of carbon paper. Place these on top of a piece of white railroad board. Trace over the tracing to transfer the snowman drawing on the tracing paper to the railroad board. Remove the tracing paper and carbon paper. Use felt-tip pens and colored pencils to outline and add color to the railroad board snowman drawing. Cut out the snowman and laminate. Trim the laminating film from the cut-out. On the snowman's stomach, cut two horizontal slots, approximately 2¾″ and 1″ apart. Cut the tagboard or art paper into strips 2″ x 11″ and laminate.

PROCEDURE: Think of a number of rhyming words appropriate for the grade level of the students, or see the end of this book for a list of rhyming words from which to select. Using a washable transparency pen or a dry-mark pen, write words that have rhyming words on the laminated strip. Put the word strip behind the Snowman Tachist-o-Scope, thread it through the bottom slot, then back through the top slot.

    To use, slide the word strip exposing a word. Call on a student to read the word and give one or more rhyming words. Then pull the word strip to expose the next word and call on another student to read the word and think of one or more rhyming words. Continue in this manner.

    When finished with the rhyming word practice on the Snowman Tachist-o-Scope, simply remove the word strip and wipe off the words. New words can then be written on the word strip, the word strip threaded back into the snowman, and the Snowman Tachist-o-Scope is again ready for use.

SNOWMAN TACHIST-O-SCOPE

Motivation Book Report Form

TICKETS TO THE PLOT!
(Grades 5–6)

Distribute a copy of TICKETS TO THE PLOT! to each student. After students have finished reading a library book, have them fill in the requested information on each ticket. The students can then lightly color the tickets with crayons or colored pencils.

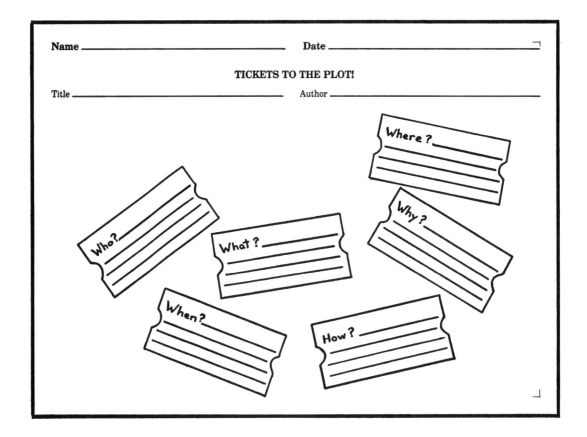

Name

TICKETS TO THE PLOT!

Title

Author

Where? _____

Why? _____

How? _____

What? _____

When? _____

Who? _____

Motivation Book Report Form

SUPER DETECTIVE STORY

(Grades 3–6)

Set up a display of mystery books appropriate for your grade level on a table in your classroom. Place copies of the motivation book report form SUPER DETECTIVE STORY on the table.

Enthusiastically point out the mystery book display to the students. Tell them that you would like them to select a mystery from the display or from the school or public library. Explain that after they have completed reading the mystery book they have selected, they should fill out the SUPER DETECTIVE STORY form. Hold up the form. Talk about the information they will fill in on each of the magnifying glasses. Then turn the students loose to select their books and begin reading!

Super Detective Story

Author

Title

How was the mystery solved?

What was the mystery?

CUDDLE UP

WITH A GOOD BOOK

READING IS

VERY APPEALING

VOCABULARY PRACTICE TRANSPARENCY

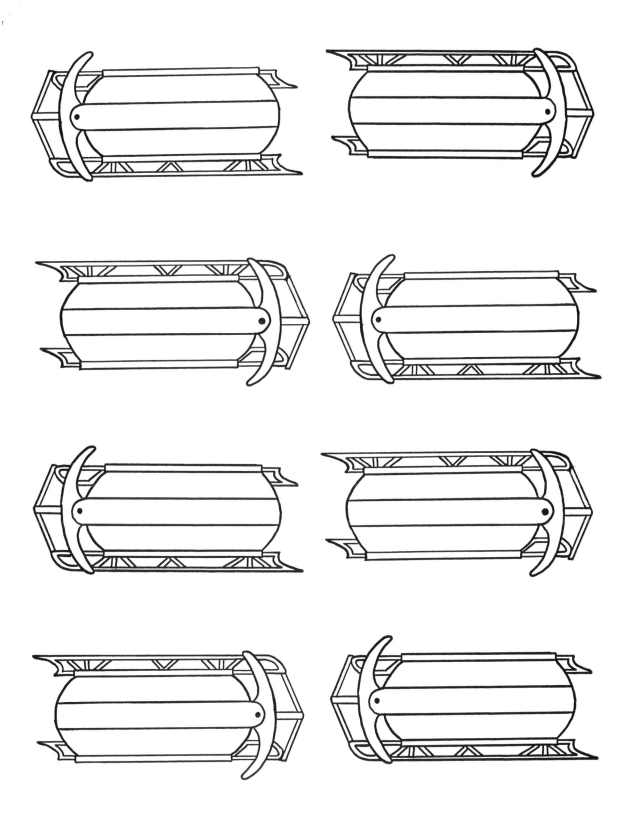

Use this page to make a transparency for developing word recognition or for vocabulary/word meaning practice. Write the words to be practiced on the sleds with a washable transparency pen.

VOCABULARY PRACTICE TRANSPARENCY

Use this page to make a transparency for developing word recognition or for vocabulary/word meaning practice. Write the words to be practiced on the snowpeople with a washable transparency pen.

Story Extension Activity

Name ——————————————— **Date** ———————————————

CHAIN OF EVENTS

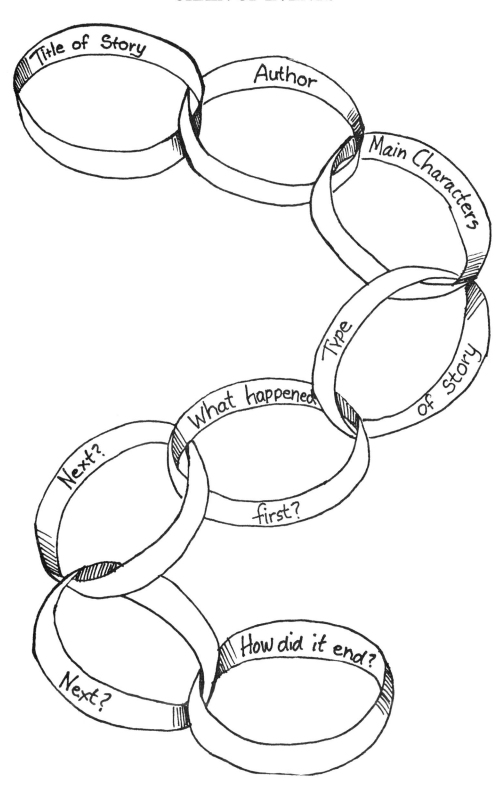

Story Extension Activity

Name _____ **Date** _____

IF I HAD BEEN THE AUTHOR

Title of story _____

Author _____

Characters in the story _____

Briefly tell about the story. _____

_____

_____

_____

What would have happened if one of the characters had acted differently? How would that have changed the story?

_____

_____

_____

_____

_____

_____

_____

Reading Motivation Bulletin Board

BE COOL . . . READ A BOOK!

(Grades 1–6)

PURPOSE: Reading motivation

MATERIALS: —light-blue bulletin board paper
—white bulletin board paper
—bulletin board pattern
—permanent ink felt-tip markers (assorted colors)
—colored pencils (assorted colors)
—scissors
—stapler
—cellophane tape or masking tape
—opaque projector (or overhead projector)

PREPARATION: Cover a bulletin board with light-blue bulletin board paper. Use an opaque projector to project the caption lettering onto the bulletin board. Trace the lettering onto the bulletin board with a black felt-tip marker.

Tape a large sheet of white bulletin board paper to a chalkboard. (You may wish to tape a couple sheets of newspaper behind the bulletin board paper to absorb any felt-tip marker ink that might soak through the bulletin board paper.) Next, using an opaque projector, project the bulletin board picture onto the white paper. Trace the picture with a permanent ink, black felt-tip marker. Then color in the picture appropriately with the markers and colored pencils. Cut out the polar bear on the iceberg and staple it onto the bulletin board.

NOTE: If an opaque projector is not available, make a transparency of the bulletin board. Then, using an overhead projector, project the illustration onto the bulletin board paper and trace.

BE COOL
READ A BOOK!

FEBRUARY

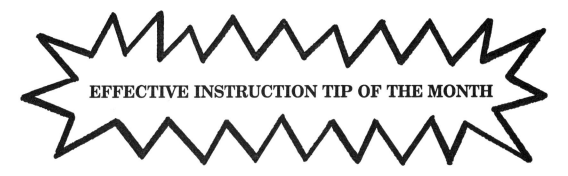

EFFECTIVE INSTRUCTION TIP OF THE MONTH

KEEP STUDENTS ACTIVELY INVOLVED

When self-checking reading workbook pages or duplicator pages in a reading group, students are frequently inattentive. Often the teacher will call on one student to read a workbook question and give the correct answer and then will call on the next student to read the next one and give the answer. Many students' minds disengage during this type of activity.

To stamp out wandering minds and to assure that students are really following along and thinking about and checking their own answers on the page, try this simple technique. Call on one student to give an answer. Have the rest of the students signal "thumbs up" if they have the same answer, "thumbs down" if they do not have the same answer. This forces every student to pay attention to every answer. You should then confirm that the answer is correct and briefly tell why, or, if the student's answer is incorrect, call on another student to give the correct response. Be sure to always briefly explain the reasoning behind the correct answer to provide corrective input to those students who did not know or were unsure of the correct answer.

Of course, if many students are indicating that they have the wrong answer, you should take time to explain in more depth. Sometimes you may even need to take time out right then and there to reteach the skill upon which the workbook page is based.

THE VALENTINE GAME

(Grades 1–6)

PURPOSE: Word recognition/word meaning

(*Variations*: synonyms, antonyms, rhyming words, consonants, consonant blends, vowels, prefixes, suffixes)

MATERIALS: —sheet of pink or red railroad board or posterboard
—The Valentine Game gameboard
—permanent, black felt-tip marker
—black fine-line marker
—white felt-tip marker
—white-colored pencil
—scissors
—paper fastener
—paper clip
—unlined white file cards
—laminating materials
—paper cutter
—game markers

PREPARATION: Using an opaque projector, reproduce the gameboard on a sheet of pink or red railroad board or posterboard with the permanent, black felt-tip marker. Color the pathway of hearts and the cupid white using the white felt-tip pen for the hearts and the white-colored pencil for the cupid. Print the game directions on the reverse side of the gameboard, if desired. Laminate the gameboard.

To make the spinner, cut out a small heart from the railroad board or posterboard. Using the black felt-tip pen, divide the heart into three sections. Write a numeral in each section. Laminate. Then punch a hole through the center of the heart. Insert a paper fastener through a paper clip, then through the hole in the center of the heart. Bend the prongs of the paper fastener, leaving it somewhat loose so that the paper clip will spin easily.

Cut 2″ x 3″ cards from the unlined white file cards. Select vocabulary words for word recognition practice or word meaning practice from the reading book. Print a different word on each card.

You will also need three or four markers.

GAME DIRECTIONS: The game is played by two to four players. The cards are shuffled and placed face down on the "Put Cards Here" box on the gameboard. The game markers are placed on the START heart. The first player spins the spinner and moves a marker forward the indicated number of spaces, draws a card, pronounces the word, and tells the meaning. If the player cannot correctly pronounce the word or tell its meaning, he/she must move his/her marker back one space. It is then the next player's turn to spin the spinner, etc. The WINNER is the first player to land on the FINISH heart.

LOLLIPOP WORD PRACTICE

(Grades 1–2)

PURPOSE: To develop recognition of new vocabulary words in the reading lesson

MATERIALS: pieces of colored railroad board or posterboard (assorted colors)
—compass to make circles
—Popsicle™ sticks
—rubber cement
—scissors
—laminating materials
—black dry-mark pen or transparency pen

PREPARATION: Using a compass, draw circles with 2½″ diameters on various colors of railroad board or posterboard. Cut out the circles and laminate them. Using rubber cement, glue a Popsicle™ stick to the back of each circle. The lollipops are now complete and ready for words to be written on them.

Using a black transparency pen or dry-mark pen, print the new words for the reading lesson on the lollipops, one word per lollipop.

PROCEDURE: Use the lollipops to introduce the new words for the reading lesson to a reading group. After introducing the words with the lollipops, place the lollipops face down on the table and have students take turns selecting a lollipop and reading the word on it.

The lollipops can be used again and again with different reading lessons and different reading groups. Simply wipe off the words and write on new ones for the next lesson on the next reading group.

CONTRACTION COOKIES

(Grades 2–6)

PURPOSE: Knowledge of contractions

MATERIALS: —tan construction paper
—manila envelope or decorative wallpaper envelope
—one 5″ × 8″ unlined file card
—Contraction Cookie patterns
—photocopier or duplicator machine
—black Flair pen
—rubber cement
—scissors
—permanent, black felt-tip marker
—laminating materials
—X-Acto™ knife
—black dry-mark pen or black transparency pen

PREPARATION: Photocopy or duplicate the Contraction Cookie Pattern Page onto tan construction paper to make 12–32 cookies. The actual number of Contraction Cookies you make should depend on the grade level/attention span of the students. Use a black Flair pen to outline the border of each cookie and to color the chocolate chips. Cut out each cookie. Select the contractions to be practiced in the activity from the list provided at the back of this book. Write a different non-contracted form of a contraction on the back of each cookie. Leave one cookie blank.

Next, make an Answer Key so students can self-correct their work on completion of the activity. On an unlined 5″ × 8″ file card, write the non-contracted form and the contraction for each of the non-contracted forms used on the cookies. Then laminate all of the cookies except the blank cookie. Also, laminate the Answer Key.

Glue the one unlaminated cookie to the front of a manila envelope with rubber cement. Using a permanent, black felt-tip marker, print the activity title, CONTRACTION COOKIES, on the front of the envelope. On the back of the envelope, write the directions, "Write the contractions on the cookies. Then check your answers with the Answer Key." Laminate the manila envelope with the flap open. Then carefully slit the envelope opening with an X-Acto™ knife. Then fold down and crease the envelope flap. Place the contraction Cookies and the Answer Key in the activity envelope.

A black dry-mark pen or a washable black transparency pen will also be needed for this activity.

PROCEDURE: This activity can be done independently or in pairs. Using a black dry-mark pen or a washable black transparency pen, students write the contractions beneath the non-contracted forms on the back of each cookie. After completing the activity, students check their own work by pulling out the Answer Key from inside the activity envelope and comparing the answers. After checking the answers, student answers are wiped off of the cookies and the Contraction Cookies are ready for the next student(s).

Front   Back

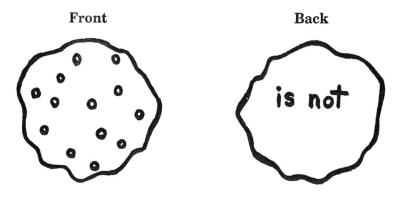

CONTRACTION COOKIES PATTERN PAGE

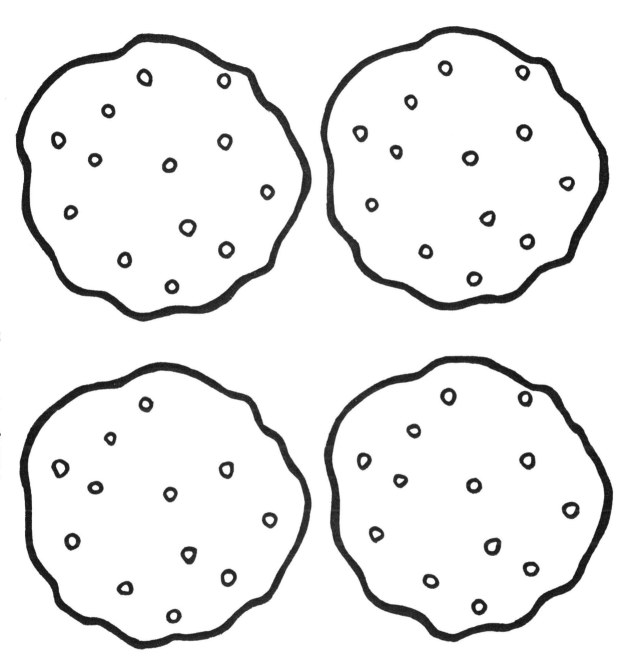

SYNONYM FLIP

(Grades 2–6)

PURPOSE: Vocabulary/word meaning development

MATERIALS: —red posterboard

—4 notebook rings—1½″ diameter

—5″ × 8″ yellow unlined file cards

—black felt-tip marker

—black Flair pen

—colored pencils—assorted colors

—paper cutter

—paper punch

—laminating materials

PREPARATION: Cut the red posterboard to make two pieces, 4″ × 8″ in size. Print *SYNONYM FLIP* on one of the pieces. Using the paper cutter, cut yellow unlined file cards to make 30 to 40 3″ × 3½″ cards. Select vocabulary words that have synonyms from past reading lessons. Using the black Flair pen, print the selected words and the synonyms on the cards, one word per card.

Next, make the activity self-correcting by putting identical color dots on the matching synonym cards. The color dots for different pairs should vary in color, position, and/or pattern.

Laminate the synonym cards and the two pieces of red posterboard. Sort the word cards into two piles so that the vocabulary words are in one pile and the matching synonyms are in another pile. Mix up the order of the words in the synonym pile. Then, use a paper punch to punch two holes about an inch apart near the top of each of the vocabulary word cards. Punch two holes in an identical manner in each of the corresponding synonym cards. Punch four holes in the piece of posterboard with the activity title *SYNONYM FLIP* and in identical spots on the second piece of posterboard. Make sure the holes you punch in the two pieces of posterboard line up exactly with the holes on the vocabulary cards and the synonym cards when the two sets of cards are placed inside the two pieces of posterboard.

Now, place the two sets of cards inside the two pieces of posterboard, with the posterboard piece with the activity title *SYNONYM FLIP* on top. Place the cards with the vocabulary words on the left side and the synonym cards on the right side. Put the four notebook rings through the four sets of holes and snap the rings together. You now have a terrific, self-correcting vocabulary reinforcement activity ready for student use.

PROCEDURE: The student looks at the first vocabulary word card on the left side of the activity, then looks through the cards on the right side to find the matching synonym. When the student thinks the matching synonym has been found, he or she looks at the back of the two cards. If they have identical color dots (same color, same location, same pattern), the two cards are synonyms. The student continues through the vocabulary cards in this manner, finding the synonyms and checking the answers.

BONUS IDEA OF THE MONTH

FANTASTIC ENVELOPES FOR LEARNING GAMES AND ACTIVITIES

You can easily make attractive, inviting-looking, simply fantastic Manila envelopes to hold match-up activities or game pieces.

MATERIALS: —wallpaper sample book
—manila envelope
—scissors
—rubber cement
—pencil
—permanent felt-tip marker

PREPARATION: Obtain a discontinued wallpaper sample book from a wallpaper store. Many wallpaper stores give away these wallpaper sample books free to teachers. Other stores sell them for a dollar or two. They come in different sizes. Select a large one containing vinyl wallpaper samples.

Next, you will need a manila envelope to use as a pattern. A 6″ × 9″ envelope is a nice size for match-up activity parts and game pieces. However, you can choose larger or smaller ones if you wish. Carefully pick the manila envelope open at the two seams on the back of the envelope, the one at the bottom of the envelope and the one up the center. Next, select an attractive piece of wallpaper from the sample book. Remove it from the book. Lay it reverse side up and place the opened up, flaps spread out, manila envelope on top of it. Using a pencil, trace the outline of the opened up manila envelope onto the piece of wallpaper. Cut the wallpaper along the pencil outline of the manila envelope. Now, take the wallpaper envelope that you have cut out and fold it, right side out, the way the original manila envelope was folded to begin with, starting with the left flap. Crease along that fold. Now do the same with the right side flap. Next, rubber cement the two flaps together just as the original manila envelope had been glued. Now fold up, crease, and glue the bottom flap. The final step is to simply fold down and crease the top flap of the envelope—no glue this time.

Your decorative manila envelope is now ready for your learning activity, game, or game pieces to be placed inside. All that remains is to print the title of the activity on the front of the envelope with a permanent felt-tip marking pen.

These envelopes are so durable, so attractive, and so easy and cheap to make, you'll never buy a plain, old manila envelope again!

BEST FRIENDS TACHIST-O-SCOPE
(Grades 1–4)

PURPOSE: Word recognition or word meaning
(*Variations*: letter-sound relationships, synonyms, antonyms, rhyming words, prefixes, suffixes)

MATERIALS: —white railroad board or posterboard
—Best Friends Tachist-o-Scope
—white tagboard or heavy white art paper
—pencil
—permanent, black fine-line marker
—permanent felt-tip markers—assorted colors
—colored pencils—assorted colors
—scissors
—tracing paper
—carbon paper
—laminating materials
—art knife
—washable transparency pen or dry-mark pen

PREPARATION: Trace the Best Friends Tachist-o-Scope pattern onto a sheet of tracing paper. Place the tracing paper on top of a sheet of carbon paper. Place these on top of a piece of white railroad board or posterboard. Trace over the tracing to transfer the kitten and puppy drawing on the tracing paper to the railroad board. Remove the tracing paper and the carbon paper. Use a permanent, black fine-line marker to outline the drawing. Use colored pencils and felt-tip markers to color the kitten and puppy attractively. Cut out the Best Friends Tachist-o-Scope and laminate. Trim the laminating film from the cut-out. Using the art knife, cut two horizontal slots, approximately 2″ long and 1″ apart on the front of the cutout. Cut the tagboard or art paper into strips 2″ × 11″ and laminate.

PROCEDURE: Select vocabulary words for sight word recognition practice or word meaning development. Using a washable transparency pen or dry-mark pen, print the words on the laminated strip, one beneath the other and approximately 1″ apart. Put the word strip behind the Best Friends Tachist-o-Scope and thread it through the bottom slot, then back through the top slot.

To use, slide the word strip up exposing a word. Call on a student to read the word or read the word and tell what it means. Then pull the word strip up to expose the next word and call on another student to read the word. Continue in this manner.

When finished with the word recognition practice with the reading group, simply remove the word strip and wipe off the words with a damp paper towel. New words can then be written on the word strip and the Best Friends Tachist-o-Scope is ready for use with the next reading group.

Motivation Book Report Form

THE ABCDEFG'S OF A GOOD BOOK
(Grades 3–6)

Distribute a copy of THE ABCDEFG's OF A GOOD BOOK to each student. After students have finished reading a library book, have them write a book report on this motivational book report form. When they have finished filling in the information, have them color in the letters A, B, C, D, E, F, and G going down the page and in the title with colored pencils, crayons, or felt-tip markers.

The completed book reports can be displayed for other students' viewing.

Name _____ Date _____

THE **ABCDEFG'S** OF A GOOD BOOK

Author _____

Book title _____

Characters _____

_____

_____

Describe where the story took place. _____

_____

_____

Explain what happened in the story. _____

_____

_____

_____

Fine ending? Tell about it. _____

_____

_____

_____

Great book? What made it so good? _____

_____

_____

_____

Motivation Book Report Form

Name _____ **Date** _____

THE **ABCDEFG'S** OF A GOOD BOOK

Author _____

Book title _____

Characters _____

_____

_____

Describe where the story took place. _____

_____

_____

_____

Explain what happened in the story. _____

_____

_____

_____

Fine ending? Tell about it. _____

_____

_____

_____

Great book? What made it so good? _____

_____

_____

_____

VOCABULARY PRACTICE TRANSPARENCY

Use this page to make a transparency for developing word recognition or vocabulary/word meaning practice. Write the words to be practiced on the valentine hearts with a washable transparency pen.

VOCABULARY PRACTICE TRANSPARENCY

Use this page to make a transparency for developing word recognition or vocabulary/word meaning practice. Write the words to be practiced on the dinosaurs with a washable transparency pen.

Story Extension Activity

Name _____   **Date** _____

STORY WORD SEARCH

Skim through the story you have just read.
Find words to fill in each of the hearts.

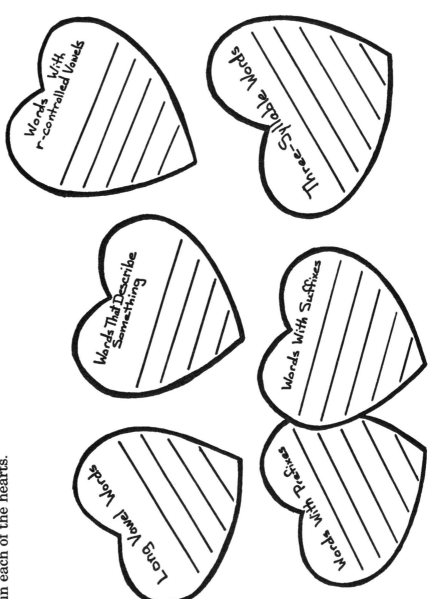

Words With r-controlled Vowels

Three-Syllable Words

Words That Describe Something

Words With Suffixes

Long Vowel Words

Words With Prefixes

Name _____ **Date** _____

MY FAVORITE CHARACTER

Title of story _____ Author _____

Draw a picture of your favorite character from the story you have just read.

Character's name _____

What is special about this character? _____

_____

_____

_____

_____

_____

Reading Motivation Bulletin Board

PUT SOME MAGIC IN YOUR LIFE

(Grades 1–6)

PURPOSE: Reading motivation

MATERIALS: —yellow bulletin board paper
—white bulletin board paper
—bulletin board pattern
—permanent-ink felt-tip markers (assorted colors)
—colored pencils (assorted colors)
—scissors
—stapler
—cellophane tape or masking tape
—opaque projector (or overhead projector)

PREPARATION: Cover a bulletin board with yellow bulletin board paper. Use an opaque projector to project the caption lettering onto the bulletin board. Trace the lettering onto the bulletin board with a felt-tip pen.

Tape a large sheet of white bulletin board paper to a chalkboard. (You may wish to tape a couple sheets of newspaper behind the bulletin board paper to absorb any felt-tip marker ink that might soak through the bulletin board paper.) Next, using an opaque projector, project the bulletin board picture onto the white paper. Trace the picture with a permanent-ink, black felt-tip marker. Then color the picture with the markers and colored pencils. Cut out the picture and staple it onto the bulletin board.

NOTE: If an opaque projector is not available, make a transparency of the bulletin board. Then, using an overhead projector, project the illustration onto the bulletin board paper and trace.

PUT SOME MAGIC IN YOUR LIFE...

READ A BOOK!

MARCH

EFFECTIVE INSTRUCTION TIP OF THE MONTH

DEVELOPING A LIFELONG LOVE OF BOOKS AND READING

It is important that we avoid making the basal reader the be-all and end-all of our reading program. It was never intended to be the entire reading program, but rather the core of instruction. Effective classroom teachers of reading extend beyond the reading book to hook students' interest in reading. They make sure their students love to read!

To extend beyond the reading book and to foster the love of books and reading in your students, you will want to:

1. *Read to your students every day.* This is probably the #1 best way to promote the love of books and reading! Class schedules are always full, with so much to teach and so little time in the school day. But no matter how tight the time schedule, it is very important that you find time—indeed, make time—to read to your students.

   Students of all ages love to have a story read to them. The teacher who makes time to read aloud is proving to each and every child in the classroom that books are great, that the stories contained in them are delightful, and that reading is highly rewarding. Frequently, the characters and plots of great books read aloud to students become lasting memories for the students. The enjoyment of the books lasts on and on!

2. *Encourage your students to read library books for pleasure.* Reading the stories in the basal reading textbook is just the start of reading. Students should be expected to read for pleasure in self-selected library books every day. Whenever they have free time they should automatically be getting out their library books and continuing on with a story almost too good to put down.

   The teacher sets the tone of how students will use free time. Teachers who make it clear to students that free time is reading pleasure time will have students who are eager to grab a library book and read whenever possible.

You may also wish to institute Sustained Silent Reading (SSR) on a daily basis in your classroom. In SSR, a specific 15-minute period is set aside daily. During that time, all students and the teacher sit and read silently.

3. *Set an example. Let students see you reading for pleasure.* Let them see you chuckling with enjoyment when you come to a good part in a book you are reading to yourself. Your obvious pleasure in reading will be perceived by the students. It will impact on their perception of books and reading.

4. *Talk up books!* Tell students about some of the book characters that were your favorites when you were their age. Pick up library books displayed in the classroom and talk enthusiastically about them. Find opportunities to remind them of some of their favorite characters from books you have read aloud to the class.

5. *Have lots of books displayed attractively in your classroom.* Make it easy for a child to be enticed by a book!

6. *Use a "bait and lure" technique.* Read the first couple chapters of a good book aloud to the class. Then place the book on display and watch students clamor to get the book and finish reading it to themselves!

7. *Consider purchasing sets of paperback books.* With these on hand, you can occasionally take a reading group out of the basal reading book and have them read and discuss as a group a paperback book.

Kindling in your students a lifelong love of books should be a major goal. The example you set, the enthusiasm you radiate, the easy access you provide, and the orientation toward books you convey will have a lasting impact on many of your students.

Multi-Purpose Gameboard

LUCKY SHAMROCKS
(Grades 1–6)

PURPOSE: Multi-purpose: letter recognition, letter sound relationships, sight word recognition, definitions, synonyms, antonyms, rhyming words

MATERIALS: —14″ × 22″ sheet of green railroad board or posterboard
           —Lucky Shamrocks gameboard
           —permanent, black felt-tip marker
           —colored pencils
           —scissors
           —laminating materials
           —game markers
           —die

PREPARATION: Using an opaque projector, reproduce the gameboard on the 14″ × 22″ sheet of green railroad board or posterboard with the black felt-tip marker. Use colored pencils to add color to the leprechaun and to the pot of gold. Print the game directions on the reverse side of the gameboard, if desired. Laminate the gameboard. With the permanent, black felt-tip marker, print different words or letters on each circle of the gameboard pathway depending on the skill the game is to reinforce.

    You will also need three or four markers and a die.

> *NOTE: To change the words or letters on the laminated gameboard pathway, simply spray with hair spray and wipe off the words/letters with a tissue. The gameboard pathway will then be erased and ready for new words or letters again to be written on the laminated surface with a permanent felt-tip marker. This simple technique makes it easy to change the skill being reinforced on the gameboard!*

GAME DIRECTIONS: The game is played by two to four players. The object of the game is to take the leprechaun to his pot of gold. The game markers are placed on the leprechaun. The first player throws the die and moves a marker forward the indicated number of spaces, and performs the task (i.e., pronounces the word and says a rhyming word, names a word that begins with the specified consonant blend, etc.) for the space upon which he/she landed. If the player cannot perform the task, he/she must move his/her marker back one space. It is then the next player's turn to throw the die, etc. The WINNER is the first player to land on the pot of gold.

Lucky Shamrocks

RACING CARS

(Grades 1–6)

PURPOSE: To develop word recognition and/or word meaning of new vocabulary words in the reading lesson

MATERIALS: —heavy white art paper or white tagboard
—washable felt-tip markers (assorted colors)
—black Flair pen
—Racing Car patterns
—photocopier or duplicator machine
—laminating materials
—scissors
—black dry-mark pen or transparency pen

PREPARATION: Duplicate or photocopy the racing car patterns onto heavy white art paper or onto white tagboard. Using the washable felt-tip markers, color the racing cars. Then trace over all of the lines on each car with the black Flair pen. Laminate and cut out each of the racing cars.

PROCEDURE: Using a black dry-mark pen or a transparency pen, print a different vocabulary word from the reading lesson on each racing car.

Now you are ready to use the cards to introduce and drill on new vocabulary words in the reading lesson. First, introduce the new vocabulary words in the manner indicated in the teacher's manual for the basal reading program you are using. Then use the racing car cards as fun flash cards to reinforce recognition or word meaning of those new words.

When the instructional activity is completed, wipe off the words and write new words for the next reading group or for the next lesson.

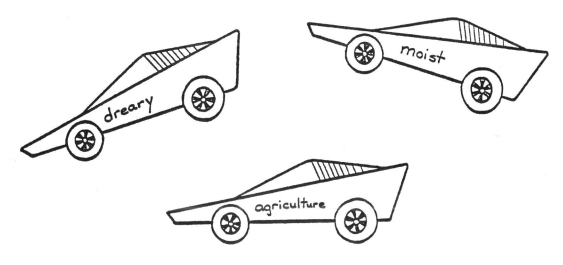

RACING CARS PATTERN PAGE

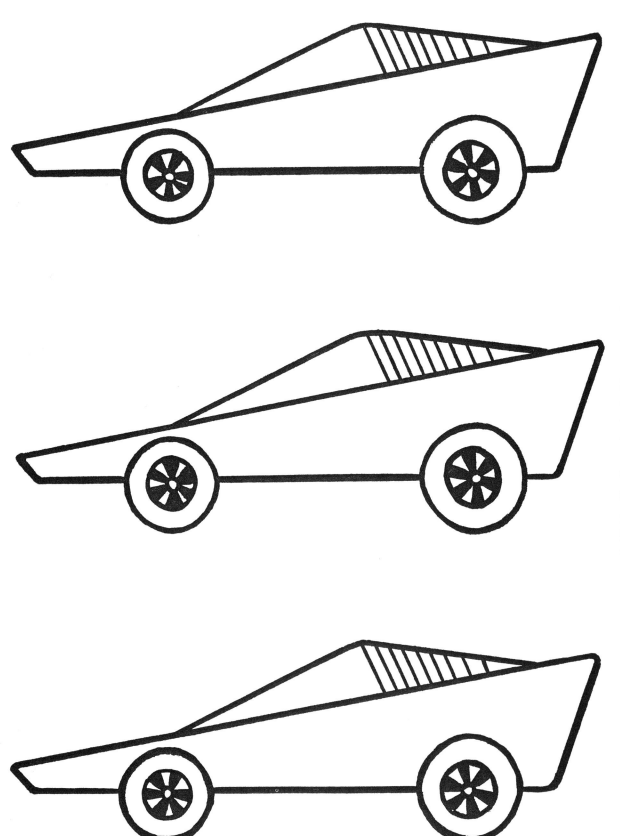

SILENT STARS

(Grades 4–6)

PURPOSE: Recognize silent letters in *gn*, *kn*, *wr*, and *mb*

MATERIALS: —yellow construction paper or yellow coverstock
  —Silent Stars patterns
  —black Flair pen
  —duplicator machine or photocopier
  —scissors
  —laminating materials
  —red dry-mark pen or transparency pen
  —box
  —attractive self-stick vinyl
  —black, permanent-ink felt-tip marker

PREPARATION: Photocopy or duplicate the Silent Stars Pattern onto sheets of yellow construction paper or yellow coverstock. Outline each star with a black Flair pen. Cut out the stars.

Select words containing *gn*, *kn*, *wr*, and *mb* from the listing in the Word Bank below. The words selected should be appropriate to the reading level of the students. Print a different word on each star with the black Flair pen.

Word Bank					
gnaw	sign	knot	wrestle	wrist	plumb
gnarled	know	knowledge	wreath	wrong	bomb
gnat	knew	knitting	wrench	wring	comb
gnome	knee	knit	wren	write	crumb
gnu	knife	knelt	wrap	thumb	limb
design	kneel	knight	wreck	numb	tomb
resign	knock	wrinkle	wrote	dumb	

Laminate the stars. Then, place them in a box covered with attractive self-stick vinyl paper and print the activity title, SILENT STARS, on the top of the box with a permanent, black felt-tip pen. Add a red dry-mark pen or red transparency pen to the contents of the box.

PROCEDURE: Using the red dry-mark pen or transparency pen, have students individually or in pairs draw a line through the silent letter(s) in each word. When the student or pair of students has completed striking out the silent letters, check to see that student(s) has/have marked each word correctly. Then have the student(s) wipe off the marks on the stars and the activity is ready for the next child or pair of children.

VOCABULARY POSTERS

(Grades 1–6)

PURPOSE: Word recognition/word meaning

MATERIALS: —12″ × 18″ sheets of heavy white art paper or oaktag

           —old magazines and catalogs

           —black Flair pens or similar fine-line markers

PREPARATION: List on the chalkboard 8–12 vocabulary words that have been recently introduced to the students but to which the students need further exposure in order to master the word recognition and/or word meaning. Place a stack of old magazines and catalogs in an easily accessible location. Place nearby several black Flair pens or similar fine-line markers.

PROCEDURE: Distribute a 12″ × 18″ sheet of heavy white art paper or oaktag to each student. Have the students look through the old magazines or catalogs to find pictures to illustrate the vocabulary words listed on the chalkboard. Have them cut out the pictures, glue them on the poster paper, and label them to make attractive vocabulary posters. Display the completed vocabulary posters.

BONUS IDEA OF THE MONTH

WORDS ON HANDS

Every teacher has some students who cannot remember sight words from one day to the next. Here is a terrific technique, highly effective in helping those children recall and retain those sight words!

MATERIALS: washable, *non-toxic*, black felt-tip marker
PREPARATION: None
PROCEDURE: Keep a washable, *non-toxic*, black felt-tip marker handy at the reading table when working with the below-average reading group. When a student is reading aloud and comes to a word he/she doesn't know, tell the child the word and let him or her continue reading until the end of his or her turn. If the word missed is a word the child should have known, but is having difficulty remembering, have the child open his/her hand, palm side up. Then print the word on the child's hand and tell the child the word you printed. Have the child look carefully at the word and say it aloud to you. Explain to the child that you want him/her to remember it because you are going to ask him/her to tell you that word later.

Continue on with the story, printing selected words on the hands of students who miss a word. After you have finished with that reading group, take a minute and have each student show you the word(s) on his/her hand and tell you the word before sending the students back to their desks. Then, off and on throughout the day, whenever you walk by the desk of a student with a word on his/her hand, reach down, gently open the student's hand and softly ask what the word is. When the students line up to go out for recess, quietly ask various students to name the word(s) on their hands. Out at recess or in the cafeteria, when convenient, gently open up the hands of various students and ask them to name the word. By the end of the day those students will indeed know the words on their hands!

NOTE: If you teach remedial reading, you can also use the technique effectively. Simply put the children's classroom teachers up to asking the children to name the words on their hands off and on throughout the day. You can also put the other students in the remedial reading group to helping each other by asking each other what their word is.

This technique is highly effective and the students love it! The only problem with the technique is that the students will love it so much that they will beg for more and more words on their hands; one on each finger of one hand, one on each finger of both hands. You will have to be careful to only put a couple of words on the hand(s) of a student each day. If you get tempted to put too many words on a child's hands in one day, the child will be unable to learn them all and both you and the child will become frustrated. Remember, a little bit of a good thing is all that is needed. One or two words per day thoroughly learned by a child with retention difficulty is better than NO words learned!

LEPRECHAUN TACHIST-O-SCOPE

(Grades 1–6)

PURPOSE: Word recognition
   (*Variations*: letter-sound relationships, synonyms, antonyms, rhyming words)

MATERIALS: —white railroad board or posterboard
   —white tagboard or heavy white art paper
   —Leprechaun Tachist-o-Scope
   —pencil
   —black fine-line marker
   —permanent felt-tip markers—assorted colors
   —colored pencils—assorted colors
   —scissors
   —tracing paper
   —carbon paper
   —laminating materials
   —art knife
   —washable transparency pen or dry-mark pen

PREPARATION: Trace the Leprechaun Tachist-o-Scope pattern onto a sheet of tracing paper. Place the tracing paper on top of a sheet of carbon paper. Place these on top of a piece of white railroad board or posterboard. Trace over the tracing to transfer the leprechaun drawing on the tracing paper to the railroad board. Remove the tracing paper and the carbon paper. Use a black fine-line pen and/or black felt-tip pen to outline the drawing. Color the leprechaun and pot of gold attractively using the felt-tip markers and colored pencils. Cut out the leprechaun and pot of gold and laminate. Trim the laminating film from the cut-out. Using the art knife, cut two horizontal slots, approximately $2\frac{3}{4}''$ long and $1''$ apart on the pot of gold. Cut the tagboard or art paper into strips $2'' \times 11''$ and laminate.

PROCEDURE: Select vocabulary words for word recognition practice in a reading group lesson. Using a washable transparency pen or dry-mark pen, print the sight words on the laminated strip, one beneath the other and approximately $1''$ apart. Put the word strip behind the Leprechaun Tachist-o-Scope and thread it through the bottom slot, then back through the top slot.

   To use, slide the word strip up exposing a word. Call on a student to read the word. Then pull the word strip up to expose the next word and call on another student to read the word. Continue in this manner.

   When finished with the word recognition practice with the reading group, simply remove the word strip and wipe off the words with a damp paper towel. New words can then be written on the word strip and the Leprechaun Tachist-o-Scope is ready for use with the next reading group.

LEPRECHAUN TACHIST-O-SCOPE

Motivation Book Report Form

FANTASY!
(Grades 4–6)

Display an assortment of fantasy books on a table in the classroom or along the chalkholder of the chalkboard. Your school librarian or the children's librarian at your local public library can help you select good fantasy books your students will enjoy.

Discuss with the students what fantasy is. Give examples of familiar books that fit into this category. Let the students think of other examples.

Point out to the students the display of fantasy books. Enthusiastically talk about some of the individual books in the display. Talk about some of your favorites. Talk it up so that the children are absolutely itching to read a fantasy book!

Explain to the students that you would like each of them to select a fantasy book, either from the display or from the library. Distribute a copy of the motivation book report form, FANTASY, to each student. Explain that after they have finished reading a book, they are to write a book report on this form.

The completed book report forms can be colored lightly and then displayed on a wall or a bulletin board. Students can read each other's book reports and select additional books to read based on those reports.

Name _____   **Date** _____

FANTASY!

Title

Author

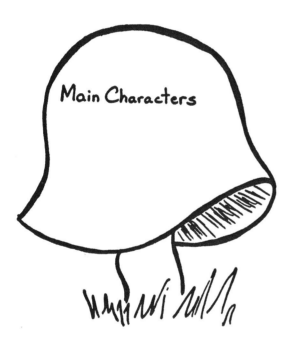

Main Characters

What was the
story about? _____
_____
_____
_____
_____
_____
_____
_____
_____

How could you tell this book was fantasy? _____

_____

_____

_____

_____

_____

Motivation Book Report Form

SCIENCE FICTION AND SCIENCE FANTASY
(Grades 5–6)

Display an assortment of science fiction and science fantasy books on a table in the classroom or along the chalkholder of the chalkboard. Your school librarian or the children's librarian at the local public library can help you select good science fiction and science fantasy your students will enjoy.

Discuss with the students what constitutes science fiction and science fantasy. Give some examples of books that fit into the categories and with which the students would be familiar. Let the students think of other examples. You may also want to point out examples of movies that are science fiction and science fantasy, including *Star Trek* and *Star Wars*.

Point out the display of science fiction and science fantasy books. Enthusiastically talk about some of the individual books in the display. "Sell" the children on the fun of science fiction and science fantasy!

Explain to the students that you would like each of them to select a science fiction or science fantasy book, either from the display or from the library. Distribute a copy of the motivation book report form SCIENCE FICTION AND SCIENCE FANTASY to each student. Explain that after they have read a science fiction or science fantasy book, they are to write a book report on this sheet.

The completed activity sheets can be colored lightly and then displayed on a wall or a bulletin board.

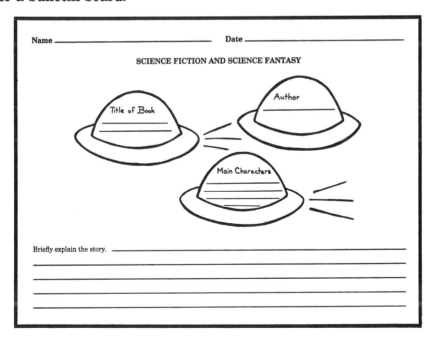

Name _____

Date _____

SCIENCE FICTION AND SCIENCE FANTASY

Author _____

Title of Book _____

Main Characters _____

Briefly explain the story. _____

_____

_____

_____

_____

VOCABULARY PRACTICE TRANSPARENCY

Use this page to make a transparency for developing word recognition or for vocabulary/word meaning practice. Write the words to be practiced on the gold coins with a washable transparency pen.

VOCABULARY PRACTICE TRANSPARENCY

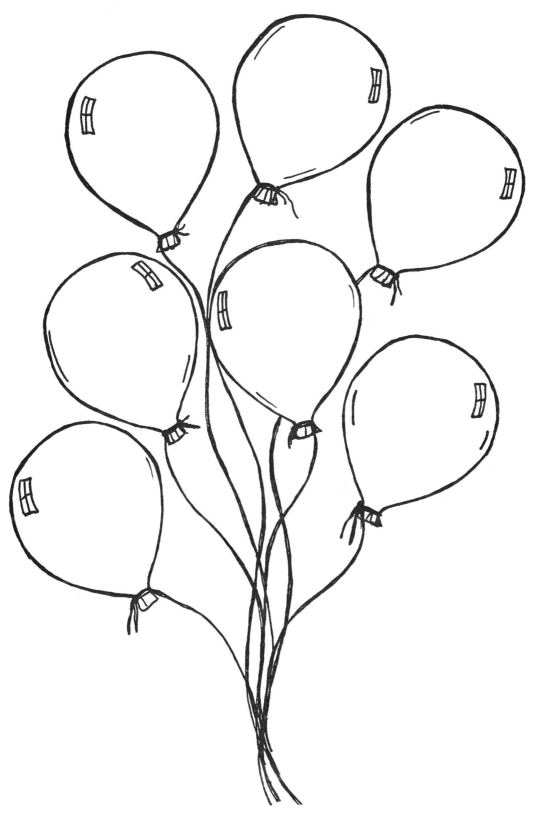

Use this page to make a transparency for developing word recognition or for vocabulary/word meaning practice. Write the **words to be practiced** on the balloons with a washable transparency pen.

Name ———————————————— **Date** ————————————————

WHAT A BIOGRAPHY!

Title of story ———————————————— Author ————————————————

    Select a character from the story. Invent a biography about that character. Include information on the character's life from the time of his/her birth until the time the story took place. Use your imagination and develop an interesting biography.

Name of story character: ————————————————————————————

Biography: ————————————————————————————————

———————————————————————————————————————

———————————————————————————————————————

———————————————————————————————————————

———————————————————————————————————————

———————————————————————————————————————

———————————————————————————————————————

———————————————————————————————————————

———————————————————————————————————————

———————————————————————————————————————

———————————————————————————————————————

———————————————————————————————————————

———————————————————————————————————————

———————————————————————————————————————

———————————————————————————————————————

———————————————————————————————————————

———————————————————————————————————————

Continue your biography on another sheet of paper.

Name _____ **Date** _____

MORE ADVENTURES OF . . .

Title of story _____ Author _____

    Pick a character from the story. Write a new story about that character, telling an entirely new happening.

Name of character: _____

_____

_____

_____

_____

_____

_____

_____

_____

_____

_____

_____

_____

_____

_____

_____

_____

Continue your story on another sheet of paper.

Reading Motivation Bulletin Board

RISE ABOVE THE ORDINARY

(Grades 1–6)

PURPOSE: Reading motivation

MATERIALS: —light-blue bulletin board paper
—bulletin board pattern
—white bulletin board paper
—permanent felt-tip markers (assorted colors)
—colored pencils (assorted colors)
—scissors
—stapler
—cellophane tape or masking tape

PREPARATION: Cover a bulletin board with light-blue bulletin board paper. Use an opaque projector to project the caption lettering onto the bulletin board. Trace the lettering onto the bulletin board with a felt-tip marker.

Tape a large sheet of white bulletin board paper to a chalkboard. (You may wish to tape a couple sheets of newspaper behind the bulletin board paper to absorb any felt-tip marker ink that might soak through the bulletin board paper.) Next, using an opaque projector, project the bulletin board picture onto the white paper. Trace the picture with a black felt-tip marker. Then color in the picture with the markers and colored pencils. Cut out the hot air balloon and staple it onto the bulletin board.

NOTE: *If an opaque projector is not available, make a transparency of the bulletin board pattern. Then, using an overhead projector, project the illustration onto the bulletin board paper and trace.*

APRIL

HOLIDAY BOOKS FOR CHILDREN TO READ AND ENJOY

Below is a list of Easter-related and Passover-related books with *approximate* independent reading grade levels indicated. Check with your school librarian or the children's librarian at your local public library for more excellent books for the holidays. You may wish to create a special springtime reading center with flowers and stuffed animals to display these books. Or, you may wish to simply place them along the chalkholder of your chalkboard where children will easily see them and be lured to pick them up and read them.

Many of these books also lend themselves to being read aloud by the teacher. Without question, the time you spend reading aloud to your students is invaluable. Reading aloud to your students improves their reading and vocabulary skills and increases their desire to learn to read and their enjoyment of books.

THE APRIL RABBITS—David Cleveland	(1–2)
HAPPY EASTER, DEAR DRAGON—Margaret Hillert	(1–2)
SILLY TILLY AND THE EASTER BUNNY—Lillian Hoban	(1–2)
HOW SPIDER SAVED EASTER—Robert Kraus	(1–2)
THE EASTER BUNNY—Winfried Wolf	(1–3)
THE GOLDEN EGG BOOK—Margaret Wise Brown	(1–3)
EASTER PARADE—Mary Chalmers	(1–3)
BUNCHES AND BUNCHES OF BUNNIES—Louise Mathews	(1–3)
LITTLE RABBIT'S BABY BROTHER—Fran Manushkin	(1–3)
THINGS TO MAKE AND DO FOR EASTER—Marion Cole and Olivia H.H. Cole	(2–4)
THE COUNTRY BUNNY AND THE LITTLE GOLD SHOES—DuBose Heyward	(2–4)
PETOOK—Caryll Houselander	(2–4)
MISS SUZY'S EASTER SURPRISE—Mariam Young	(2–4)
THE EASTER EGG ARTISTS—Adrienne Adams	(2–4)
HUMBUG RABBIT—Lorna Galian	(2–4)
THE CHOCOLATE RABBIT—Maria Claret	(2–4)
EASTER TREAT—Roger Duvoisin	(2–4)
THE BIG BUNNY AND THE EASTER EGGS—Steven Kroll	(2–4)
THE BIG BUNNY AND THE MAGIC SHOW—Steven Kroll	(2–4)
MOUSEKIN'S EASTER BASKET—Edna Miller	(2–4)
A TALE FOR EASTER—Tasha Tudor	(2–4)
THE BUNNY WHO FOUND EASTER—Charlotte Zolotow	(2–4)
BUNNY TROUBLE—Hans Wilhelm	(2–4)

OUT WITH ROUND ROBIN READING, IN WITH DIRECTED ORAL READING

Round robin reading, the technique in which students take turns reading aloud one after another around a table or up and down the aisles, has some definite weaknesses in grades 3–6. Remember back when you were in elementary school as a student? You must have had a teacher or two who used this technique. Do you remember what you did while you were waiting for your turn to read? Of course you do. You counted the number of students yet to read before you, then you counted the number of paragraphs and determined the paragraph or paragraphs you would be asked to read. Then you sat there and practiced to yourself the paragraph(s) you would have to read. You weren't following along with the story being read! And what happened after you finished your turn of reading aloud? You didn't have to pay attention anymore. You were off the hook. You could daydream if you chose to do so and no one would be the wiser.

Round robin reading, while it can be justified at first grade, and to some extent at second grade, is simply not an effective instructional technique at third grade and up. It actually encourages students not to pay attention to the story line and it allows them to disengage from the instructional activity.

Many teachers justify round robin reading by saying that it helps children develop oral reading skills or because it provides an opportunity for them to diagnose difficulties a child may be having. Sometimes teachers will justify using this technique because they believe it is a way of making sure students who won't read the story silently when it is assigned will read it.

There is another, far superior, instructional technique that provides an opportunity for teachers to listen to the students read aloud, strongly promotes reading comprehension skills, keeps students actively involved throughout the lesson, and conveys strongly to the students that they had better have read the story silently before the reading group meets or they will be "out of it" during reading group time. What is this incredible alternative technique? It is an instructional technique called the "directed oral reading lesson."

The procedure for implementing the directed oral reading lesson is very easy. Using your normal instructional procedure, introduce the new story in the reading book and teach the new vocabulary words according to the teacher's manual. Then assign the story to be read by the students at their seats. The next day, instead of reading the story using the round robin technique, ask the group a comprehension question about the story. Then ask them to skim down through the first page (or first two pages) to find the sentence or paragraph that contains the answer to the question. Have them raise their hands when they have found the answer. After a number of students have their hands up, call on a student to read orally the sentence or paragraph that contains the answer. As the rest of the students listen to the designated student read, they are either thinking "Great! I had the right answer," or "That answer isn't right. The sentence I found had a better answer." If the designated student has selected the correct section to provide the answer to the question, indicate that the answer is correct and discuss why, then beam another question to the group and continue on in this pattern. If the designated student has not selected the correct response, ask the rest of the students if someone has found a different sentence or paragraph to answer the question and call on another student.

Some questions you will ask will be literal questions with one sentence or one paragraph in the story providing the correct answer. Other questions you will ask will be more open-ended, with a number of different sentences or paragraphs providing evidence of the answer. When you ask an open-ended question, be sure to let students read aloud the several different sentences or paragraphs they have found.

Coming up with the questions to ask the group in this type of lesson is very easy. Simply use the questions found in the Teacher's Manual of your reading program. The teacher's manual will have a reduced student text page, then beneath it, comprehension questions that go with that page. This will provide you with questions that actually go with a certain page of text and will allow you to tell the students the page to skim to find the answer to the question you have just asked. It will also provide you with questions on a variety of thinking levels.

Now let's take a minute to analyze the difference in student involvement and student learning in a directed oral reading lesson. Using this method, all students are actively involved in skimming the story to find the answer to each question. To find a sentence or paragraph they think may have the answer, they must use critical thinking skills. When a student is called on to read the material containing an answer to a question, oral reading skills are being developed. As the rest of the students listen to the student called on to read his or her passage, each one is critically evaluating his or her answer, determining whether they agree with the student, whether their answer is incorrect, or whether the answer they have is better than the one given.

In addition, any student who has not already read the story silently is going to have difficulty quickly skimming to locate answers to the questions. They are going to feel uncomfortable and out of it. If you use this technique regularly, these students will quickly get an unstated message that they had better read that story before reading group!

In comparing the difference in degree of student involvement and comprehension skill development between the directed oral reading lesson and the round robin reading lesson, it is quite obvious that directed oral reading is far superior. It is effective and easy to implement. If you have been using round robin reading, now is the time to switch. Try it, you'll like it!

Multi-Purpose Gameboard

BUNNY TRAIL
(Grades 1–6)

PURPOSE: Multi-purpose: letter sound relationships, sight word recognition, synonyms, antonyms, rhyming words, syllabication, definitions

MATERIALS: —14″ × 22″ sheet of yellow railroad board or posterboard
   —Bunny Trail gameboard
   —permanent, black felt-tip marker
   —black Flair pen or similar fine-line marker
   —colored pencils—assorted colors
   —black Stanford's Sharpie pen
   —hair spray
   —scissors
   —game markers
   —die

PREPARATION: Using an opaque projector, reproduce the gameboard on the 14″ × 22″ sheet of yellow railroad board or posterboard with the black felt-tip marker and the black Flair pen. Use the colored pencils to color the resulting picture attractively. Print the game directions on the reverse side of the gameboard, if desired. Laminate the gameboard. With the permanent-ink, black Sharpie pen, print different words or letters on each egg along the game pathway depending on the skill the game is to reinforce.

   You will also need three or four markers and a die.

NOTE: To change the words or letters on the laminated gameboard pathway, simply spray with hair spray and wipe off the words/letters with a tissue. The gameboard pathway will then be erased and ready for new words or letters to be written on the laminated surface with permanent marker. This simple technique makes it easy to change the skill being reinforced on the gameboard.

GAME DIRECTIONS: The game is played by two to four players. The object of the game is to follow the Easter Bunny trail from the upper left corner of the gameboard where it says START to the lower right corner where it says FINISH. The game markers are placed on the START position. The first player throws the die and moves the marker forward the indicated number of spaces and performs the task (e.g., pronounces the word and says a synonym, names the vowel and says a word that contains that vowel) for the space upon which he or she has landed. If the player cannot perform the task, his or her marker must be moved back one space. It is then the next player's turn to throw the die. The WINNER is the first player to reach the Easter Bunny in the lower right corner of the gameboard.

COMPOUND CANOES

(Grades 2–6)

PURPOSE: Recognition of compound words

MATERIALS: —red, blue, green, yellow, and tan construction paper
—black Flair pen
—scissors
—Compound Canoes patterns
—photocopier or duplicator machine
—laminating materials
—scissors
—black dry-mark pen or black transparency pen
—box
—attractive self-stick vinyl
—black, permanent-ink felt-tip marker

PREPARATION: Duplicate or photocopy the Compound Canoes patterns onto the assorted colors of construction paper indicated above to make 16–24 canoes (the number to be determined by the attention span of the students). Use a black Flair pen to outline all of the lines on each of the canoes. Then cut out each of the canoes.

Next, print a different compound word on each canoe. The compound words can be selected from reading instructional material you are using or from the list of compound words provided at the back of this book. The words selected should be at an appropriate reading level for the students.

Laminate the canoes. Then place the compound canoes in a box covered with attractive self-stick vinyl and print the activity title, COMPOUND CANOES, on the top of the box with the black, permanent-ink felt-tip marker.

PROCEDURE: Using a black transparency pen or a black dry-mark pen, have students draw lines between the two words that make up the compound word on each canoe. When a student has finished the activity, check to see that the words have been marked correctly. Then have the student wipe off the lines and the activity is ready for the next student.

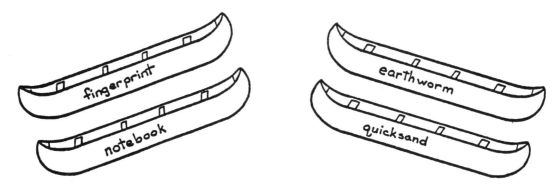

240

COMPOUND CANOES PATTERN PAGE

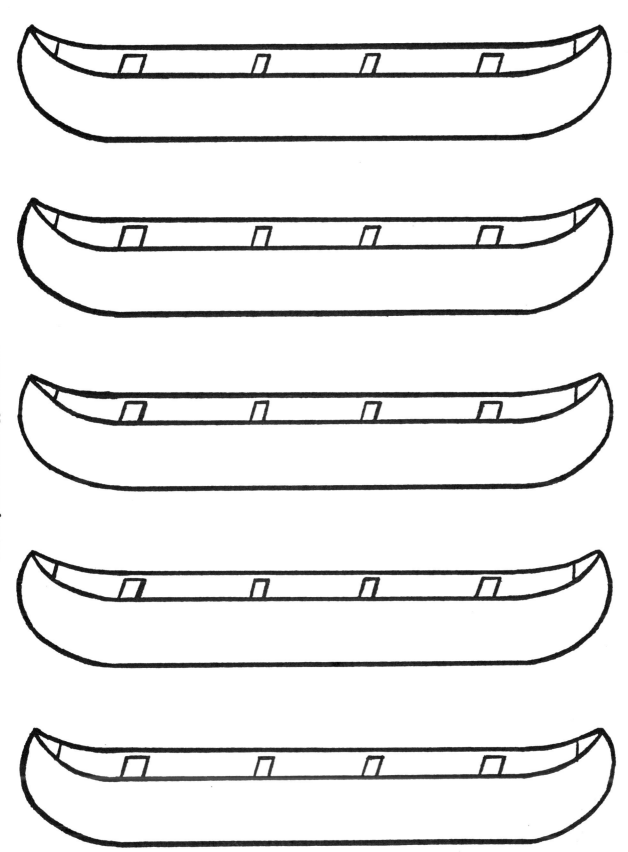

EASTER EGG HUNT

(Grades 1–6)

PURPOSE: Vocabulary: word recognition/word meaning

MATERIALS: —plastic Easter eggs (assorted colors)—one for each child plus a couple extra
    —fine-line marking pen
    —2″ × 3″ pieces of white paper
    —several bags of jelly beans

PREPARATION: Select a number of vocabulary words you want students to review from past reading lessons. Print a different word on each slip of paper. Then insert a slip of paper with a word into each plastic egg. If you have two or three reading groups in your room, each one in different reading books or in different places in a reading book, you may wish to select different words for the different reading groups. You can place the words for one reading group in one color of eggs, the words for the second group in eggs of another color, etc. In this manner, word eggs intended for specific reading groups will be color-coded.

Hide the eggs in the schoolyard or around the classroom a short time before the activity is to take place. Of course, the eggs should be hidden when the students are not around to watch.

PROCEDURE: Have the students go on an Easter Egg Hunt. Tell the students the boundaries of the search. If you have color-coded the eggs for different reading groups, assign the colors of eggs the different groups are to search for. Explain that each student is to search for and find one egg. After finding an egg, students should quickly rejoin you with their eggs in hand. They can cheer on students still searching for eggs, but they cannot provide clues as to locations of unfound eggs.

All students will probably quickly find eggs. If, however, sufficient search time has passed and a couple of students still have not found eggs, turn the whole class loose to find the remaining eggs and simply give them to the students without eggs.

Next, have the students return to their desks with their eggs. As you call on students one at a time, have them read the word on the paper inside the egg or read the word and tell its meaning. As a student reads a word or reads the word and tells its meaning, give the student several jelly beans as a prize. If a student can't read the word or read the word and give its meaning, tell the student the correct answer then tell him or her that you will come back in a minute and give him or her another chance to answer correctly. Continue on with another one or two students then return to the student who could not answer correctly. This time the student should be able to answer correctly and earn the jelly bean prize. Quickly continue in this manner around the room.

After all students have read the words on their eggs, you may wish to have the students trade eggs. Then quickly go around the room again having the students read their new words. You may wish to omit the jelly beans this time.

This activity can be used with first grade through sixth grade students. With first and second grade students the words will be sight words and students will be working on simple word recognition. At the upper grade levels, the words can be newly learned vocabulary words for which the students must recall the correct pronunciation as well as the meaning of the word.

NOTE: If you prefer to omit the jelly bean rewards, simply have the students read their words, etc., without giving out jelly beans.

BONUS IDEA OF THE MONTH

TICKET OUT

Here is a great activity that lends itself to the review and/or reinforcement of a wide variety of material and is appropriate for use in grades 1–6. The students will love it and you will, too.

MATERIALS: None.
PREPARATION: None.
PROCEDURE: Do this activity when it is time for the students to leave the room for recess, lunch period, or to go home. First, select a skill you want to review or reinforce. Some good examples of these might include: vocabulary/word meaning, vowel sounds, consonant blends or digraphs, rhyming words, synonyms, antonyms, number of syllables in a word. The possibilities are endless, limited only by your imagination. Have students line up at the door single file, ready to leave the room. Before they can leave the room, they must each give you a Ticket Out. The Ticket Out is the correct answer to the question you ask. Some examples of the many ways you can use this activity include:

1. *Short Vowel Practice*—Ask the first student in line to tell you a word that contains a short *e*. As soon as the student tells you a word that contains that short vowel, he/she may leave the room. Ask the next student in line to give you a word that contains a short *o*. Continue in this manner right on through the line of students.

2. *Consonant Blends Practice*—For the Ticket Out, each student in turn must name a consonant blend. Another way to practice consonant blends is for you to name the various consonant blends, and each student in turn must say a word beginning with the consonant blend you specify.

3. *Synonyms*—Ask the first student in line to tell you a synonym for the word you pronounce. As that student leaves the room, ask the second student for a synonym for a second word you pronounce, etc.

4. *Antonyms*—Ask the first student in line to tell an antonym for a word you pronounce, the second student, an antonym for the next word you pronounce, etc.
5. *Definitions of Vocabulary Words*—Ask the first student to give a definition of the first vocabulary word you pronounce, the second student, the definition for the second vocabulary word, etc.
6. *Number of Syllables in Words*—Ask the first student in line to tell you the number of syllables in the first word you pronounce, the second student, the number of syllables in the second word you pronounce, etc.
7. *Prefixes*—Ask the first student to tell you a word that contains the prefix you state, the second student a word for the second prefix you state, etc.
8. *Sight Word Recognition*—For this one you will need flash cards for the words to be practiced. Show each student, in turn, a flash card. Upon successfully naming the word on the card, the student leaves the room and it is the next student's turn to read correctly the word on the next flash card.

When a student cannot correctly name a word or demonstrate the skill required, tell him/her the answer. Then have the student move back one place in line. When it is that student's turn again, ask the student the same question he or she just missed. After the student answers it correctly, he or she may leave the room.

Be sure to keep this activity moving right along. Don't let it begin to drag. Students should quickly be given their question, answer quickly, and be allowed to leave the room. If a student can't give an answer, wait three seconds, tell the student the answer, and have the student move back one place in line.

Students love this activity. You will find them begging to do a Ticket Out.

BUNNY TACHIST-O-SCOPE

(Grades 1–4)

PURPOSE: Word recognition or word meaning (*Variations*: letter-sound relationships, synonyms, antonyms, rhyming words)

MATERIALS: white railroad board or posterboard
—white tagboard or heavy white art paper
—Bunny Tachist-o-Scope
—pencil
—black fine-line marker
—permanent felt-tip markers—assorted colors
—colored pencils—assorted colors
—scissors
—tracing paper
—carbon paper
—laminating materials
—art knife
—washable transparency pen or dry-mark pen

PREPARATION: Trace the Bunny Tachist-o-Scope pattern onto a sheet of tracing paper. Place the tracing paper on top of a sheet of carbon paper. Place these on top of a piece of white railroad board or posterboard. Trace over the tracing to transfer the bunny drawing on the tracing paper to the railroad board. Remove the tracing paper and the carbon paper. Use a black fine-line pen to outline the drawing. Use the colored pencils and Magic Markers to color the Bunny Tachist-o-Scope attractively. Cut out the bunny and laminate. Trim the laminating film from the cut-out. Using the art knife, cut two horizontal slots, approximately 2″ long and 1″ apart on the front of the bunny. Cut the tagboard or art paper into strips 2″ × 11″ and laminate.

PROCEDURE: Select vocabulary words for sight-word recognition practice or word meaning development. Using a washable transparency pen or dry-mark pen, print the words on the laminated strip, one beneath the other and approximately 1″ apart. Put the word strip behind the Bunny Tachist-o-Scope and thread it through the bottom slot, then back through the top slot.

To use, slide the word strip up exposing a word. Call on a student to read the word or read the word and tell what it means. Then pull the word strip up to expose the next word and call on another student to read the word. Continue in this manner.

When finished with the word recognition practice with the reading group, simply remove the word strip and wipe off the words with a damp paper towel. New words can then be written on the word strip and the Bunny Tachist-o-Scope is ready for use with the next reading group.

BUNNY TACHIST-O-SCOPE

Motivation Book Report Form

GOOD BOOK FOR A RAINY DAY
(Grades 4–6)

Distribute a copy of GOOD BOOK FOR A RAINY DAY! to each student. After students have finished reading a good library book, have them write a book report on this motivational book report form. When they have filled in all of the information, have them lightly color the raindrops blue with crayons or colored pencils. The completed book report forms can then be displayed on a wall or a bulletin board so that students can read each others' book recommendations.

Name _____ Date _____

GOOD BOOK FOR A RAINY DAY!

Title _____

Author _____ Type of book _____

Tell about the book: _____

_____

_____

_____

_____

Give two reasons this book is a good book for a rainy day:

1. _____

2. _____

Think of another good title for this book: _____

Name someone else you think would particularly like to read this book: _____

Name _____ Date _____

GOOD BOOK FOR A RAINY DAY!

Title _____ Type of book _____

Author _____

Tell about the book: _____

_____

_____

_____

_____

Give two reasons this book is a good book for a rainy day:

1. _____

2. _____

Think of another good title for this book: _____

Name someone else you think would particularly like to read this book: _____

VOCABULARY PRACTICE TRANSPARENCY

Use this page to make a transparency for developing word recognition or for vocabulary/word meaning practice. Write the words to be practiced on the carrots with a washable transparency pen.

VOCABULARY PRACTICE TRANSPARENCY

Use this page to make a transparency for developing word recognition or for vocabulary/word meaning practice. Write the words to be practiced on the Easter eggs with a washable transparency pen.

Name ——————————————— **Date** ———————————————

SOLVE THAT PROBLEM

Title of story ——————————————— Author ———————————————

      Pick a character from a story. Explain the problem the character had and how the character solved the problem.

Name of character: ————————————————————————————————

——

——

——

——

——

——

——

——

——

——

——

——

——

——

——

——

——

——

Reading Motivation Bulletin Board

READING MAKES ME HOP WITH HAPPINESS!
(Grades 1–6)

PURPOSE: Reading motivation
MATERIALS: —white bulletin board paper
                    —light-brown bulletin board paper
                    —bulletin board pattern
                    —one sheet heavy white art paper
                    —permanent felt-tip markers (assorted colors)
                    —colored pencils (assorted colors)
                    —scissors
                    —stapler and staples
                    —cellophane tape or masking tape
                    —opaque projector or overhead projector and transparency
                    —cotton balls (optional)
                    —white school glue (optional)
PREPARATION: Cover a bulletin board with white bulletin board paper. Use an opaque projector to project the bulletin board picture onto the bulletin board. Trace the lettering and picture, except the rabbit, onto the bulletin board paper with felt-tip markers.

Tape a large sheet of brown bulletin board paper to a chalkboard. (You may wish to tape a couple of sheets of newspaper behind the bulletin board paper to absorb any felt-tip marker ink that might soak through the bulletin board paper.) Next, using an opaque projector, project the picture of the rabbit onto the brown paper. Trace the rabbit, minus its tail, onto the paper with a black felt-tip marker. Then attach a piece of heavy white art paper to the chalkboard and trace the rabbit's tail with the marker. Next, cut out the rabbit and the rabbit tail.

Staple the rabbit onto the bulletin board. Then staple the white tail onto the rabbit. (VARIATION: If you want to use a "cotton tail" instead of a white paper tail for the rabbit, glue cotton balls onto the white paper tail before attaching the tail to the bulletin board.)

NOTE: If an opaque projector is not available, make a transparency of the bulletin board pattern. Then, using an overhead projector, project the illustration onto the bulletin board paper for tracing.

READING MAKES ME "HOP" WITH HAPPINESS!

MAY/JUNE

SANITY SAVERS: TECHNIQUES TO REFOCUS STUDENT ATTENTION

May is here, and students are thinking about summer vacation. Indeed, some students may be acting as though summer vacation is beginning tomorrow. This is a hard time to keep students' attention focused on the reading lessons and assignments. Yet the month of May may represent as much as one-ninth of the learning time in the school year. It is a shame to let the month slip by with minimal learning taking place because students, eagerly anticipating vacation, are not paying much attention.

In addition to keeping the reading lessons interesting, there are some techniques that will help you refocus student attention when minds begin to wander. These techniques can be used all year long, but can be absolutely teacher sanity-savers in May and early June.

One technique is that of touch. When you are working with a reading group around a table and see a child's mind begin to wander, simply reach over and touch the child's hand or arm. This will immediately bring the child's attention back to the group. Ask the child a lesson-related question that he or she will definitely be able to answer, then remove your hand. There is no need to scold the child for not paying attention. Your hand touching the child's hand or arm is all that is needed. Think of all the nagging, scolding, and unpleasantness avoided!

Another technique is to use the child's name in the explanation, the example, or the discussion. As soon as the child's name is used, his or her wandering attention will snap back to whatever you were saying. Let's imagine a typical reading group lesson. You look up and see that a boy named John Wilson has obviously started to daydream or has started to whisper to the boy next to him. In either case he is not paying attention to the lesson. To bring his attention back to the lesson by simply using his name, you might say:

1. (*lesson on syllabication in progress*)

"Let's see if we can figure out how many syllables are in John Wilson's last name. Listen to the name Wilson. How many syllables do you hear, Judy? John, do you agree that there are two syllables in your last name? Wow! We are getting good at figuring out how many syllables are in a word. Let's try another word. . ."

2. (*discussion of one of the Amelia Bedelia stories is in progress*)

"If John Wilson were Amelia Bedelia's employer, do you think he would be as patient with Amelia Bedelia's mistakes?" (Discussion follows and John Wilson will certainly be paying attention and eagerly involved in the discussion.)

It is so easy to weave the name of the student into the lesson. And it is such an easy and positive way to bring the child's attention back to the group. It certainly beats the sour taste and negative feelings of nagging, scolding, or sarcasm!

A third way to bring a child's mind back to the lesson involves the use of proximity. It simply involves walking over to and standing beside the child who has started to daydream or to misbehave in some way. Your standing beside the child will immediately bring the child's attention back or stop the misbehavior. You don't need to say a thing to the child, just stand beside him or her for a minute or two then slowly walk on. If you are in the middle of an explanation when you notice a child beginning to act up, continue right on with the explanation as you move to the child's side. Continue the lesson while you stand beside the child. The technique is truly effective. Try it, you will love it!

In addition to these techniques, you will want to make heavy use of the group response techniques suggested in the October Effective Instruction Tip of the Month.

While 100% attention 100% of the time is impossible, use of these techniques will increase student attention to the reading lesson as the days wind down to vacation. And by increasing student attention, you are maximizing student reading skill development. All this and a pleasant classroom atmosphere, too!

FROGS AND LILY PADS

(Grades 1–6)

PURPOSE: Multi-purpose match-up activity.
(Examples: Matching capital and lower case letters, vowel sounds, synonyms, antonyms, homonyms, rhyming words, contractions, or words to definitions)

MATERIALS: —large, white index cards or white posterboard/railroad board
—Frog and Lily Pad Pattern Page
—permanent Magic Markers (assorted colors)
—black, permanent, fine-line Magic marker
—scissors
—laminating materials

PREPARATION: Using the patterns, reproduce frogs and lily pads in quantity needed. Color frogs, lily pads, and lilies with Magic Markers. Laminate and cut out each piece. Using a black, thin-line, permanent Magic Marker, write letters or words on the frogs and the corresponding letters or words on the lilly pads.

Note: This activity can be made self-correcting by writing a different numeral on the reverse side of each frog and the same numeral on the reverse side of the lily pad that matches the frog. When a child has completed the activity, the frogs and lily pads can be turned over to see if the numerals on the reverse side of the matched frogs and lily pads are identical.

PROCEDURE: Have students match frogs to corresponding lily pads.

259

FROG AND LILY PAD PATTERN PAGE

MUSHROOM MAGIC

(Grades 1–6)

PURPOSE: To use context clues to figure out unknown words

MATERIALS: —white tagboard or heavy white art paper
—watercolor felt-tip markers, assorted colors
—black Flair Pen (or other fine-line marker)
—mushroom patterns
—duplicator machine
—laminating materials
—scissors
—colored pencils, assorted colors

PREPARATION: Duplicate the mushroom patterns onto white tagboard or heavy white art paper. Using the watercolor markers or the colored pencils, color each of the mushroom caps. Red, orange, light tan, pale green, light blue, and yellow caps are good color possibilities. The mushroom stems can be left white, colored to match the mushroom cap, or can be colored a contrasting color. Next, use the black Flair Pen to outline each of the mushrooms.

Write a different sentence on each mushroom, omitting one word in each sentence and drawing a line in its place. You can make up the sentences for the activity, select them from the reading textbook, or select sentences at an appropriate level of difficulty from the context clue sentences provided at the end of this book. Laminate the mushrooms.

PROCEDURE: Remind the students that any time they come to a word they don't know as they are reading along in a book, there is a "magic" way to figure out the word. All they have to do is read the rest of the sentence, then go back and reread the sentence, figuring out the unknown word by thinking what would make sense in the sentence and looking at some of the letter clues in the unknown word.

Then, show the students the Mushroom Magic activity. Explain that this activity will help them practice using clues in the sentence to figure out an unknown word. Tell them they are to do this activity as an independent

activity. They will need a sheet of paper, a pencil, and the mushrooms to do the activity. They should read the sentence on a mushroom, noting the missing word in the sentence. They should use context clues to determine a word that would make sense in the sentence. Then they should write the sentence on the sheet of paper, filling in the missing word in the sentence. They should follow the same procedure for each mushroom. When they have completed the entire activity, they should put their paper with their sentences on your desk for you to check.

MUSHROOM MAGIC PATTERN PAGE

LADYBUG CHALLENGE

(Grades 3–6)

PURPOSE: Recognize the number of syllables in words

MATERIALS: —red construction paper
—black Flair Pen
—Ladybug Challenge patterns
—duplicator machine
—laminating materials
—scissors
—black dry-mark pen or black transparency pen
—box
—solid-color self-stick vinyl
—permanent, black felt-tip marker
—white-colored pencil

PREPARATION: Duplicate the Ladybug Challenge Pattern Page onto red construction paper to make a number of ladybugs. Use a black Flair Pen to outline each of the ladybugs and to blacken all of the dark areas on the ladybugs. Use a white-colored pencil to white in the tops of the ladybugs' eyes. Then, cut out each of the ladybugs.

Next, select a number of one-, two-, three-, and four-syllable words appropriate to the reading level of the students. Laminate the ladybugs. Turn each of the ladybugs over and, using the Flair Pen, print a different word on each ladybug. Then place the ladybugs in a box covered with self-stick vinyl and print the activity title LADYBUG CHALLENGE on the top of the box with a permanent, black felt-tip marker.

PROCEDURE: Students do this activity independently. First, they pick up a ladybug, turn it over, read the word printed on it, and decide how many syllables the word contains. Then they turn the ladybug back over and, using

Front

Back

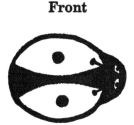

264

a black dry-mark pen or a black transparency pen, they draw black dots on the ladybug to show the number of syllables in the word found on that ladybug.

When the student has completed the activity, check the student's work. Then have the student wipe off the dots and the activity is ready for the next student.

NOTE: This activity can be made self-correcting. Simply make an Answer Key and place it in the activity box or keep it on your desk where students can refer to it when they have completed the activity.

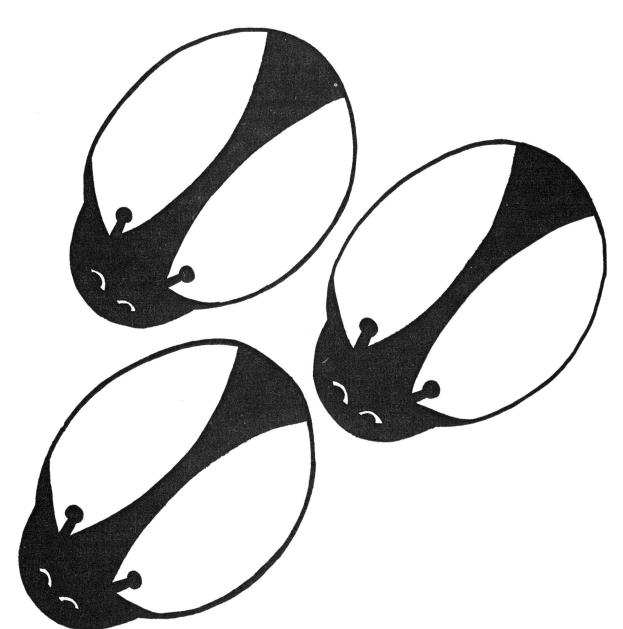

FINGERPAINTED WORDS

Here is a fun method for helping students in the primary grades and remedial reading classes quickly learn new sight words. It involves having the students fingerpaint the words to be learned! The children will love it!

MATERIALS: —fingerpaints

—fingerpaint paper or shelf paper, one sheet for each student

—water

PREPARATION: Prepare the fingerpainting area. Select a couple of words you wish students to learn. Print them on the chalkboard.

PROCEDURE: Give each student a piece of fingerpaint paper or shelf paper. Place a couple of spoonsful of fingerpaint on each student's paper. Have the students smear the fingerpaint over the surface of the paper. Then draw the students' attention to the first word you have written on the chalkboard. Tell them what the word is. Use it in a sentence, then repeat the word. Next, have the students print the word in the fingerpaint using their index finger as their "pencil." Have them say the word softly to themselves as they print it. Use the same procedure with the other words you have selected.

Point out to the students that if they make a mistake, they can "erase" it by rubbing over the word with their hand to smooth out the paint, then they can print the word again correctly. If the fingerpaint begins to dry too quickly, sprinkle a couple of drops of water onto the students' papers and let them gently smear it around.

When the students are finished writing their words, have them set their papers on the floor in an out-of-the-way spot to dry.

SUMMER READING ACTIVITIES CALENDARS
(Primary and Intermediate Levels)

Summer vacation is rapidly approaching. While summer vacation is great fun for our students, it is also a time when some of the skills learned during the school year are lost from lack of use. Unfortunately, students who do not read during the summer will probably return to school in the fall with weaker reading skills.

We need to encourage our students to read during the summer. We also need to encourage them to do other reading-related activities to help maintain or increase their skills. Providing students with a Summer Reading Activities Calendar will encourage many of your students to continue reading and doing reading-related activities during the summer.

Two levels of a Summer Reading Activities Calendar have been provided, a primary level and an intermediate level. Select the level appropriate for your grade. Then make a photocopy of each of the three pages for that level. Next, fill in the dates for the current year for each of the three months. Next, using Liquid Paper or some similar type of typewriter erase fluid, white out each of the activities on the day blocks not actually in the month on that particular year. The Summer Reading Activities Calendar has now been custom-tailored to the current school year. Reproduce the three calendar pages in sufficient quantities, staple them together in sets, and distribute them to the students sometime during the last week of school.

As you distribute the Summer Reading Activities Calendar to your students, explain that you want them to continue reading super books during the summer and doing other fun reading-related activities. Enthusiastically talk up the activities on the calendar pages. Send your students home from school that afternoon highly motivated to do the activities. Then pat yourself on the back, knowing you have done the best you can to motivate your students during the summer vacation.

NOTE: Each year the dates will fall on different days of the week so you will have to re-do the calendar each year using the same directions given above.

SUMMER READING ACTIVITIES CALENDAR

JUNE

Primary Level

Sunday	Monday	Tuesday	Wednesday	Thursday	Friday	Saturday
Enjoy a good book!	Read a book to someone younger than you.	Find a quiet place and read a good book.	Read aloud to a grown-up.	Draw pictures of words that begin with *th*.	Make a picture book showing what you would like to do this summer.	Read a story to one of your parents.
Ask someone to read a bedtime story to you.	Visit the library and select some new books.	Get wrapped up in a good book!	Draw pictures describing 8 words that have a short e sound. Then label the pictures.	Read a book under the sheets tonight using a flashlight.	Write a picture book showing your favorite animals in the world.	Borrow a good book from a friend. Return it when you have finished reading it.
Read a story to yourself.	Draw a picture of your best friend. Then write a story telling about your friend.	Pick a good book and ask someone to read it to you.	Cut out a picture from a magazine. Glue it on a piece of paper. Then write about it.	Read a book this morning. Read another book this afternoon.	Make a list of foods you like to eat.	Read a book with a friend.
Tell someone about a story you have read.	Draw pictures of 8 words that have a short i sound. Then label the pictures.	Create a bookmark then use it.	Curl up with a good book.	Read a good book to your mom. Practice reading it aloud first.	Ask someone to read a bedtime story to you.	Find a quiet place and read a good book.
Take a book to bed with you and read it before you fall asleep.	Color a coloring book picture. Then label each of the objects in the picture with the beginning sound of the object.	Read a book to a friend.	Trade books with a friend.	Draw a picture of a baby bear. Then write a story about it.	Read two picture books to yourself.	Select new books at the library.

SUMMER READING ACTIVITIES CALENDAR
JULY

Sunday	Monday	Tuesday	Wednesday	Thursday	Friday	Saturday
Read a story to a grandparent.	Make a list of all the colors you can think of. Have someone help you with the spelling if you need help.	Draw a picture of something you really wish you could have. Then write about it.	Read aloud to a grown-up.	Draw pictures of 8 words that have a short u sound. Then label the pictures.	Ask someone to read a bedtime story to you.	Draw a picture of the best part of a book you have read.
Read a story to a relative.	Draw a picture of a perfect treehouse. Then write about it.	Read a book to someone younger than you.	Pick a good book and ask someone to read it to you.	Tell someone about your all-time favorite book character.	Practice reading a story aloud. Then find someone to listen to you read.	Draw pictures of 4 words that begin with *wh*.
Ask a parent to tell you about his or her favorite book.	Play a rhyming game with someone. Take turns naming rhyming words.	Read a book under the sheets tonight using a flashlight.	Write a letter to a grandparent.	Draw pictures of 8 words that have a short a sound. Then label the pictures.	Ask your mom to buy a new book for you.	Borrow a good book from a friend.
Enjoy a good book!	Cut out pictures from an old catalog. Glue them on paper. Then label them.	Borrow a good book from a friend. Return it when you have finished reading it.	Ask someone to read a bedtime story to you.	Play an antonym game with someone. Take turns naming opposites.	Draw a picture of a magic ring. Then write a story about it.	Invite a friend over to spend the night. Read books together for part of the evening.
Make a list of fun things to do. Draw a picture of one of them.	Snuggle up in bed and read for fun!	Read a story to your mom while she fixes supper tonight.	Cut out a picture from a magazine. Glue it on a piece of paper. Then write about it.	Enjoy a good book!	Draw a picture of a toy you wish you had. Then write the reasons you wish you had it.	Enjoy a good book!

SUMMER READING ACTIVITIES CALENDAR

AUGUST

Primary Level

Sunday	Monday	Tuesday	Wednesday	Thursday	Friday	Saturday
Look through a catalog. See how many words you know.	Enjoy a good book!	List nice things about last year's teacher.	Tell someone about a story you have read.	Curl up and read for a half hour.	Ask a grandparent to give you a book for a birthday present.	Draw pictures of kinds of things people wear. Then label each thing.
Read a story to your father tonight.	Select new books at the library.	Ask someone to read a bedtime story to you.	Draw pictures of 5 words that begin with *ch.*	Write the alphabet in your best handwriting.	Read a book to someone younger than you are.	Help your mother make a shopping list to take to the grocery store.
Ask your grandparents to tell you about the books that were their favorites when they were your age.	Draw pictures of 8 words that have a short o sound. Then label the pictures.	Curl up with a good book.	Draw a picture of a very special puppy. Then write a story about it.	Trade books with a friend.	Curl up and read for a half hour.	Read a story to your father tonight.
Ask someone to read a bedtime story to you.	Read a book under the covers tonight using a flashlight.	Cut out 6 pictures of words that have a long e sound. Glue them on a sheet of paper.	Ask a friend if you can borrow one of his or her books to read.	Pretend you are a teacher. Write a story about what you would do on the first day of school.	Pick a good book and ask someone to read it to you.	Make a list of all of the consonant blends you can think of.
Enjoy a good book!	Draw a picture of a character from a book you have read.	Find someone younger to read to.	Cut out 6 pictures of words that have a long a sound. Glue them on a sheet of paper.	Tell someone about a story you have read.	Draw a picture of a boat. Then write a story about it.	Create a bookmark and then use it.

SUMMER READING ACTIVITIES CALENDAR
JUNE
Intermediate Level

Sunday	Monday	Tuesday	Wednesday	Thursday	Friday	Saturday
Read the comic section of the Sunday paper.	Swap books with a friend.	Write directions telling how to get from a friend's house to your house.	Read a magazine.	Write a poem about summer vacation.	Read the directions on a cake box.	Start a diary. Write in it each day.
Read a story to a younger child.	Write your own directions for making something, then have a friend follow them.	Curl up with a good book.	Invite a friend over to spend the night. Read books together for part of the evening.	Write a description of your best friend.	Make a list of words with the prefix re.	Make a shopping list for your mother to take to the grocery store.
Borrow a good book from a friend	Read a book under the sheets tonight using a flashlight.	Have a contest with a friend. See who can read the most books during the summer vacation.	Draw a picture of your favorite food. Write about it.	Make a list of some books you would like to read.	Select new books at the library.	Curl up and read for an hour.
Make a list of places you would like to go to and things you would like to see.	Read a story to a younger child.	Read all of the interesting information found in the front pages of the telephone book.	Ask a parent to tell you about his or her favorite book.	Read for an hour.	Circle all of the short vowel words on a cereal box.	Create a newspaper advertisement telling about your favorite book.
Ask a grandparent to give you a book for a birthday present.	Read a letter to the editor in today's newspaper. See if you agree with it.	Make a picture book for a preschool child.	Read the TV guide in the newspaper.	Draw a picture of yourself shipwrecked on a deserted island. Then make a list of books you would like to have with you on that deserted island.	Write a story telling what you would do if a skunk wandered into your kitchen.	Select new books at the library.

SUMMER READING ACTIVITIES CALENDAR

JULY

Intermediate Level

Sunday	Monday	Tuesday	Wednesday	Thursday	Friday	Saturday
Read a story to a grandparent.	List different breeds of dogs.	Write a secret message to a friend using a code.	Look at 5 or 6 cartoons. Then create a cartoon of your own.	Read a newspaper article aloud to a parent.	Make a poster advertising a book you have read.	See how many pairs of rhyming words you can list.
See how many pairs of antonyms you can list.	Make a list of words with the prefix *dis*.	Create a bookmark and then use it.	Write a letter to a grandparent.	Enjoy a good book!	Read the information on a detergent box. Circle any words you don't know. Then look them up.	Read a book under the sheets tonight using a flashlight.
Look at a road map. Read the information on the map.	Read an interesting article in a newspaper.	Swap books with a friend.	Curl up with a good book.	Draw a picture of a pet you wish you had. Write a story about it.	Make a long list of things you would like to do. Show it to a friend.	Look through a catalog. Read the descriptions of the items shown.
Tell someone about a story you have read.	Read the grocery store advertisements in the newspaper. Circle the items you wish your mother would buy.	Get wrapped up in a good book!	Read at least another chapter or two in a good book.	Make a list of all the consonant blends you can think of.	Write a description of a place you would like to visit.	Talk Mom into buying you a new book.
Ask a grandparent to tell you about his or her favorite book.	List nice things about last year's teacher.	Enjoy a good book!	Write a letter to a friend.	Ask friends if you can borrow some of their books to read.	Use a cookbook to help Mom make something.	List makes of cars.

SUMMER READING ACTIVITIES CALENDAR

Intermediate Level

AUGUST

Sunday	Monday	Tuesday	Wednesday	Thursday	Friday	Saturday
Read the TV guide in the newspaper.	Read an article to a younger child.	See how many of the states of the United States you can list.	Read a book under the sheets tonight using a flashlight.	See how many synonyms you can think of for the word "said." List them on a sheet of paper.	With a red pencil, underline all of the three-syllable words on the front page of a newspaper.	Have a contest with a friend. See who can list the most pairs of synonyms.
Do a crossword puzzle.	Select new books at the library.	Get lost in a good book!	Find three new words in a newspaper. Look up the meanings of those words.	Read a story to an elderly person.	Make a list of all the compound words you can think of. The list should be *very* long.	Draw a picture of the best part of a book you have read.
Read a book under the covers tonight using a flashlight.	With a red pencil, underline all of the two-syllable words on the front page of a newspaper.	Swap books with a friend.	Read some information in a nonfiction book.	Tell someone about your all-time favorite book character.	Find a quiet place and read.	Make a list of at least 30 contractions.
Cut out a picture from a magazine or newspaper. Then write a story to go with it.	Create new titles for two of your favorite books.	Write a description of your favorite TV show.	Enjoy a good book!	See how many words you can think of that include the suffix -*ness*. List them.	Make a poster advertising a book you have read.	Talk Mom into buying you a new book.
Make a list of words with the prefix *un*.	Read a magazine.	Curl up with a good book.	Read a story to a younger child.	Play Scrabble with a friend.	Write a story for a younger child.	Get lost in a good book!

DINOSAUR TACHIST-O-SCOPE

(Grades 1–4)

PURPOSE: Word recognition or word meaning

> (*Variations*: letter-sound relationships, synonyms, antonyms, rhyming words)

MATERIALS: —gray or white railroad board or posterboard
—Dinosaur Tachist-o-Scope
—white tagboard or heavy white art paper
—pencil
—black fine-line marker
—colored pencils, assorted colors
—permanent felt-tip markers, assorted colors
—scissors
—tracing paper
—carbon paper
—laminating materials
—art knife
—washable transparency pen or dry-mark pen

PREPARATION: Trace the Dinosaur Tachist-o-Scope pattern onto a sheet of tracing paper. Place the tracing paper on top of a sheet of carbon paper. Place these on top of a piece of gray railroad board or posterboard (if available) or white railroad board or posterboard. Trace over the tracing to transfer the dinosaur drawing on the tracing paper to the railroad board. Remove the tracing paper and carbon paper. Use a black fine-line pen to outline the drawing. If white railroad was used, use a gray-colored pencil to color the dinosaur. Color the flowers and plants appropriately. Cut out the dinosaur and laminate. Trim the laminating film from the cut-out. Using an art knife, cut two horizontal slots, approximately 2″ long and 1″ apart on the dinosaur. Cut the tagboard or art paper into strips 2″ × 11″ and laminate.

PROCEDURE: Select vocabulary words for sight word recognition practice or word meaning development. Using a washable transparency pen or dry-mark pen, print the words on the laminated strip, one beneath the other and approximately 1″ apart. Put the word strip behind the Dinosaur Tachist-o-Scope and thread it through the bottom slot, then back through the top slot.

To use, slide the word strip up exposing a word. Call on a student to read the word or read the word and tell what it means. Then pull the word strip up to expose the next word. Continue in this manner.

When finished with the word recognition practice with the reading group, simply remove the word strip and wipe off the words with a damp paper towel. New words can then be written on the word strip and the Dinosaur Tachist-o-Scope is ready for use with the next reading group.

DINOSAUR TACHIST-O-SCOPE

Motivation Book Report Form

A WIGGLY BOOK REPORT
(Grades 3–6)

Distribute a copy of A WIGGLY BOOK REPORT to each student. After students have finished reading a library book, have them write a book report on this motivational book report form.

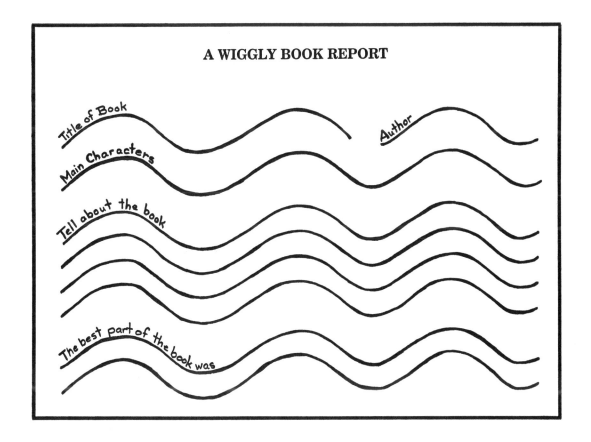

Name ——————

Date ——————

A WIGGLY BOOK REPORT

Author

Title of Book

Main Characters

Tell about the book

The best part of the book was

VOCABULARY PRACTICE TRANSPARENCY

Use this page to make a transparency for developing word recognition or for vocabulary/word meaning practice. Write the words to be practiced on the toadstools with a washable transparency pen.

VOCABULARY PRACTICE TRANSPARENCY

Use this page to make a transparency for developing word recognition or for vocabulary/word meaning practice. Write the words to be practiced on or beside the cats with a washable transparency pen.

Story Extension Activity

Name —————————————— **Date** ——————————

MY FAVORITE CHARACTER

Author ——————————

Title of story ——————————

Draw a picture of your favorite character in the story.

Write 5 words that describe this character.

1. ——————————————
2. ——————————————
3. ——————————————
4. ——————————————
5. ——————————————

Why did you like this character?

——————————————————————
——————————————————————
——————————————————————
——————————————————————
——————————————————————
——————————————————————

Character's name ——————————

Story Extension Activity

Name ——————————————— **Date** ———————————————

AROUND IT GOES!

Title ——————————————— Author ———————————————

This story was about...

Reading Motivation Bulletin Board

BOOKS ARE SOMETHING TO SING ABOUT

(Grades 1–6)

PURPOSE: Reading motivation
MATERIALS: —light-blue bulletin board paper
                     —bulletin board pattern
                     —permanent-ink, black felt-tip marker
                     —Bird and book patterns
                     —opaque projector
                     —stapler
                     —duplicator paper
                     —photocopy machine or duplicator machine
PREPARATION: Cover a bulletin board with light-blue bulletin board paper. Use
     an opaque projector to project the BOOKS ARE SOMETHING TO SING
     ABOUT bulletin board lettering onto the bulletin board. Trace the lettering
     onto the bulletin board with a permanent-ink, black felt-tip marker. Photocopy
     or duplicate the bird pattern page and distribute a copy to each student. Have
     students color their birds and cut them out. Have each child carefully print
     the title of a favorite book on the cover of the book on the pattern page, then
     cut out the book. (NOTE: If this bulletin board is being used at the first or
     second grade level, you may wish to have the students cut out the books, then
     tell you the names of their favorite books and you can print the titles on the
     books.) Students then carefully glue the books to the wings of the birds so
     that the birds take on a 3-D appearance and appear to be holding the books.
     (See the bottom of the Pattern Page for step-by-step illustrations of how to
     put the birds together.) Then, staple the birds to the bulletin board.

BIRD AND BOOK PATTERN PAGE

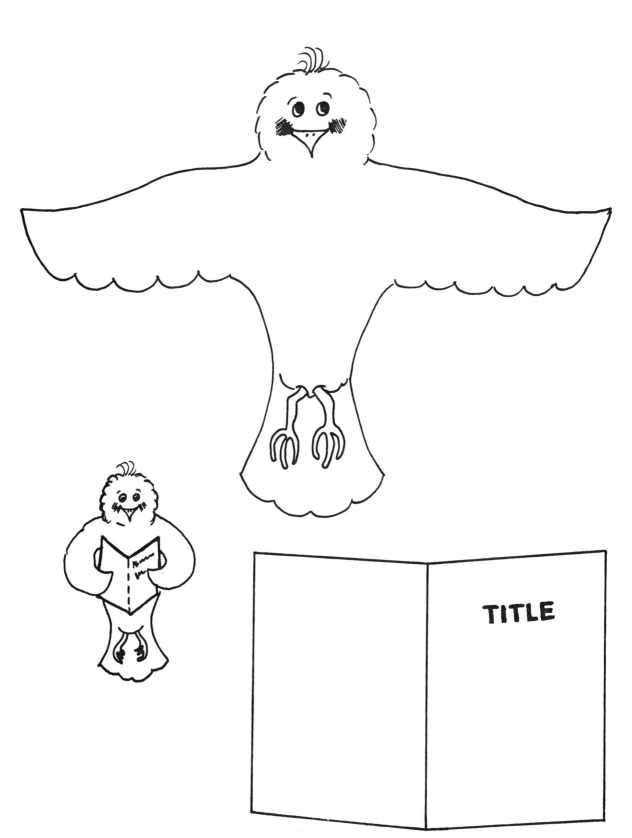

TITLE

WORD LISTS

Synonyms
Antonyms
Homonyms
Hard and Soft G Words
Figures of Speech

Contractions
Compound Words
Rhyming Words
Word Families
Context Clue Sentences

SYNONYMS

right, correct, proper, appropriate
noise, racket, commotion, clamor, uproar
mad, angry, annoyed, irritated, exasperated
mad, enraged, furious, indignant, disgusted
laugh, giggle, chuckle, snicker
hide, conceal, disguise, cover
great, magnificent, majestic, stately
funny, amusing, humorous, comical
disagree, argue, quarrel, squabble, fight
fast, rapid, swift, speedy, hasty
sparkling, glistening, glittering, gleaming
brave, bold, courageous, fearless
immense, huge, gigantic, enormous, tremendous
awful, horrible, terrible, dreadful
afraid, frightened, scared, terrified
beautiful, handsome, attractive, lovely
old, ancient, aged, antique, elderly
smart, intelligent, wise, clever, brilliant
sad, unhappy, melancholy, mournful, miserable
cranky, grouchy, cross, irritable, disagreeable
silly, absurd, ridiculous, foolish
incorrect, wrong, improper, inappropriate
weak, feeble, frail, flimsy
fat, heavy, plump, stout
wonderful, pleasant, delightful, enjoyable, marvelous
wonderful, fabulous, splendid, superb, spectacular
wet, damp, moist, soggy
trip, journey, voyage, expedition, tour
think, believe, suppose, imagine, guess
think, consider, ponder, plan
strong, sturdy, forceful, powerful
thin, skinny, slender, slim
lonely, lonesome, isolated, forlorn, desolate

ANTONYMS

in—out
over—under
open—close
little—big
old—young
old—new
boys—girls
man—woman
black—white
bald—hairy
cold—hot
on—off
wet—dry
pretty—ugly
good—bad
clean—dirty
above—below
full—empty
broken—repaired
whole—half
asleep—awake
run—walk
laugh—cry
happy—sad
smooth—rough
hard—soft
shiny—dull
light—dark
day—night
give—take
sweet—sour
sick—well
raw—cooked
frown—smile
bright—dim
easy—difficult
inside—outside
up—down
tall—short

scared—brave
wild—tame
fast—slow
future—past
fat—skinny
long—short
noisy—quiet
alive—dead
love—hate
smart—stupid
curved—straight
high—low
friends—enemies
left—right
right—wrong
win—lose
lost—found
fail—pass
fancy—plain
float—sink
rich—poor
summer—winter
spring—fall
early—late
push—pull
near—far
no—yes
add—subtract
multiply—divide
part—whole
war—peace
neat—messy
ascend—descend
brave—cowardly
over—under
many—few
friend—enemy
child—adult
light—heavy

some—none
light—dark
now—later
somewhere—nowhere
mine—yours
warm—cool
here—there
sweet—sour
huge—tiny
famous—unknown
polite—impolite
sun—moon
beautiful—ugly
enter—exit
float—sink
rainy—sunny
noisy—silent
noise—silence
healthy—ill
easy—difficult
deep—shallow
dangerous—safe
pokey—speedy
wonderful—horrible
top—bottom
windy—calm
safe—unsafe
throw—catch
grow—shrink
raw—cooked
rough—smooth
wrinkled—smooth
ceiling—floor
attic—basement
send—receive
spend—save
student—teacher
teach—learn

HOMONYMS

acts, ax
ad, add
affect, effect
aid, aide
air, heir
aisle, I'll, isle
all, awl
allowed, aloud
altar, alter
ant, aunt
arc, ark
ascent, assent
assistance, assistants
ate, eight
attendance, attendants
away, aweigh
bail, bale
bald, bawled
ball, bawl
band, banned
bare, bear
baron, barren
baroness, barreness
based, baste
bazarr, bizarre
be, bee
beach, beech
beat, beet
been, bin
bell, belle
berry, bury
berth, birth
better, bettor

billed, build
blessed, blest
blew, blue
bloc, block
boar, bore
board, bored
boarder, border
bold, bowled
bolder, boulder
burro, burrow
bough, bow
braid, brayed
brake, break
bread, bred
brewed, brood
brews, bruise
bridal, bridle
brows, browse
buy, by, bye
cache, cash
canvas, canvass
capital, capitol
carat, carrot
cause, caws
ceiling, sealing
cell, sell
cellar, seller
cent, scent, sent
cents, scents, sense
cereal, serial
chance, chants
cheap, cheep
chews, choose

chili, chilly
choral, coral
chord, cord, cored
chute, shoot
cite, sight
clause, claws
close, clothes
coarse, course
colonel, kernel
council, counsel
creak, creek
crews, cruise
currant, current
cymbal, symbol
days, daze
dear, deer
dense, dents
desert, dessert
dew, do, due
die, dye
doe, dough
draft, draught
dual, duel
ducked, duct
ewe, you
eye, I
fair, fare
feat, feet
find, fined
fir, fur
flea, flee
flew, flu, flue
flour, flower

for, fore, four
foreward, forward
forth, fourth
foul, fowl
gait, gate
gilt, guilt
gorilla, guerrilla
grade, grayed
grate, great
grays, graze
groan, grown
guessed, guest
hail, hale
hair, hare
hall, haul
halve, have
handmade, handmaid
hangar, hanger
hay, hey
heal, heel, he'll
hear, here
heard, herd
he'd, heed
higher, hire
him, hymn
hoarse, horse
hoes, hose
hole, whole
hour, our
idle, idol
in, inn
incite, insight
jam, jamb
knead, need
knew, new
knight, night
knot, not
know, no
lain, lane
laps, lapse
leak, leek
leased, least
lessen, lesson
lightening, lightning

links, lynx
loan, lone
loot, lute
made, maid
mail, male
main, Maine, mane
maize, maze
manner, manor
marry, merry
meat, meet
medal, meddle
mind, mined
miner, minor
missed, mist
moan, mown
mood, mooed
morning, mourning
necklace, neckless
none, nun
oh, owe
oar, or, ore
one, won
overdo, overdue
overseas, oversees
paced, paste
pail, pale
pain, pane
pair, pare, pear
passed, past
patience, patients
pause, paws
peace, piece
peak, peek
peal, peel
plain, plane
pleas, please
pole, poll
poor, pore, pour
praise, prays, preys
presence, presents
pride, pried
pries, prize
prince, prints
principal, principle

profit, prophet
quarts, quartz
rain, reign
raise, rays
rap, wrap
rapt, wrapped
read, red
read, reed
real, reel
residence, residents
right, write
ring, wring
road, rode, rowed
role, roll
rose, rows
sail, sale
scene, seen
sea, see
seam, seem
sew, so, sow
shone, shown
side, sighed
sighs, size
slay, sleigh
soar, sore
soared, sword
sole, soul
some, sum
son, sun
stair, stare
stake, steak
stationary, stationery
steal, steel
straight, strait
suede, swayed
suite, sweet
sundae, Sunday
tea, tee
tacks, tax
tail, tale
taught, taut
team, teem
teas, tease, tees
tense, tents

their, there, they're
threw, through
throne, thrown
tide, tied
to, too, two
toad, towed
toe, tow
told, tolled

vain, vane, vein
wade, weighed
waist, waste
wait, weight
war, wore
way, weigh
we, wee

weak, week
weave, we've
we'd, weed
who's, whose
wood, would
yoke, yolk
your, you're

HARD AND SOFT *G* WORDS

HARD *G* WORDS

gain	girl	gold
galaxy	give	golden
gale	glacier	gone
gallant	glad	good
game	gladiator	goof
gap	glamorous	gopher
garage	glare	gorilla
garden	glass	gossip
gargle	gleam	gourd
garment	gleeful	government
gas	glide	governor
gasp	glimpse	gown
gate	glisten	guarantee
gather	gloomy	guard
gazelle	glory	guess
gear	glossary	guide
get	glove	guilt
ghastly	globe	guilty
ghost	go	gum
ghoul	goat	gun
gift	gobble	guppy
giggle	goblin	gutter
gimmick	goggles	guy

SOFT *G* WORDS:

gel	gentleman	Germany
gelatin	genuine	gesture
gem	geography	giant
general	geology	ginger
generally	geometry	giraffe
generalize	George	gym
generator	geranium	gymnasium
generous	gerbil	gymnastics
genius	germ	gyp
gentle	German	gypsy

FIGURES OF SPEECH

rain cats and dogs
upset the apple cart
to kick the bucket
a bone to pick
an ax to grind
on cloud nine
once in a blue moon
to lay an egg
know the ropes
hand over fist
turn the tables
chip on one's shoulder
stick out one's neck
dead as a doornail
a wolf in sheep's clothing
fly the coop
put the cart before the horse
burn the candle at both ends
through thick and thin
to flip one's lid
bring down the house
hit the nail on the head
between the devil and the deep,
     blue sea
bark up the wrong tree
look a gift horse in the mouth
white elephant
out of the frying pan and into the
     fire
live the life of Riley
get down to brass tacks
eat humble pie
to beat the band
to cook one's goose
pay through the nose
wet blanket

fly off the handle
a chip off the old block
haul over the coals
face the music
out on a limb
a horse of another color
just under the wire
mind one's P's and Q's
let the cat out of the bag
a feather in one's cap
to talk turkey
rob Peter to pay Paul
pull the wool over one's eyes
keep the ball rolling
paint the town red
cry crocodile tears
going to town
in hot water
in the nick of time
pleased as punch
jump the gun
hold a candle to
come to the end of one's rope
from pillar to post
break the ice
sour grapes
with a grain of salt
one-horse town
eager beaver
chew the cud
a wild goose chase
to go against the grain
on one's high horse
get the lion's share
on the bandwagon
play second fiddle

take the bull by the horns
pass the buck
a fine kettle of fish
hold at bay
a red letter day
to split hairs
hanging around town
eat his words
raining cats and dogs
dropped his jaw
went in one ear and out the other
turned green with envy
hit the ceiling
follow in his footsteps
a green thumb

a bad egg
take the cake
gone to pot
get the brush-off
lame duck
put on your thinking caps
turn over a new leaf
eats like a bird
your eyes are bigger than
        your stomach
button your lip
a real blockhead
a lone wolf
on a wild goose chase

CONTRACTIONS

aren't—are not
can't—cannot
couldn't—could not
didn't—did not
doesn't—does not
don't—do not
hadn't—had not
hasn't—has not
haven't—have not
he'd—he had, he would
he'll—he will, he shall
he's—he is, he has
I'd—I had, I would, I should
I'll—I will, I shall
I'm—I am
isn't—is not
it'll—it will
it's—it is, it has
I've—I have
let's—let us
she'd—she had, she would
she'll—she will, she shall
she's—she is, she has

shouldn't—should not
that's—that is
they'd—they had, they would
they'll—they will, they shall
they're—they are
they've—they have
wasn't—was not
we'd—we had, we would, we should
we'll—we will, we shall
we're—we are
we've—we have
weren't—were not
what's—what is
who'd—who had, who would
who'll—who will
who're—who are
who's—who is, who has
won't—will not
wouldn't—would not
you'd—you had, you would
you'll—you will, you shall
you're—you are
you've—you have

COMPOUND WORDS

airline
airmail
airplane
airport
anybody
anyhow
anymore
anyone
backbone
backyard
barefoot
baseball
basketball
bathrobe
bathroom
battleship
beanbag
birthday
blackboard
bloodhound
blowup
blueprint
bookcase
bookkeeper
bookmark
boxcar
brainstorm
breakdown
broadcast
bulldog
bulldoze
bullfrog
buttercup
butterfly
buttermilk
butterscotch
campfire

carpool
catfish
checkup
classroom
clothesline
cloudburst
copperhead
copyright
cowboy
cowpuncher
crosswalk
cupcake
cutout
daybreak
daydream
daytime
dishpan
doorstep
downfall
downpour
downstairs
downtown
dragonfly
drugstore
earphone
earring
earthquake
eyeball
eyelid
farmland
filmstrip
fingernail
firearm
firecracker
firehouse
fireplace
fishhook

flagpole
flashlight
floodlight
flowerpot
folklore
folktale
football
foothill
frostbite
gentleman
gentlemen
goldfish
grapefruit
grasshopper
greenhorn
haircut
halfway
handcuff
handlebar
hardware
haystack
headache
headlight
headline
headquarters
heartbroken
highway
homemade
homesick
homework
horsefly
horseshoe
housebroken
housefly
household
housekeeper
housework

iceberg
Iceland
jellyfish
knothole
kneecap
landlady
landlord
landslide
lawsuit
leftover
lifeboat
lifeguard
lighthouse
limestone
lookout
loudspeaker
milkweed
motorcycle
mushroom
newscast
newspaper
newspring
nightgown
nightmare
notebook
oatmeal
outboard
outcome
outcry
outfield
outfit
outlaws
outside
overcoat
overcome
overlook
overpass

paperback
payoff
peanut
peppermint
pickup
pigtail
pineapple
pinpoint
playmate
playpen
ponytail
popcorn
postcard
postman
pushover
quicksand
railroad
railway
rainbow
raincoat
rattlesnake
rifleman
ripoff
roadside
rowboat
runway
sailboat
sandman
sandpaper
sawdust
scarecrow
scholarship
scrapbook
screwdriver
shellfish
shipwreck
shoelace

298

sidewalk	strawberries	thundershower	volleyball	whirlpool
silverware	starfish	thunderstorm	wallflower	whitecap
skateboard	suitcase	tiptoe	washcloth	wholesale
skyscraper	sunbeam	toadstool	washroom	wildcat
snowdrift	sunfish	toenail	wastebasket	windmill
snowstorm	sunflower	toothbrush	watchdog	windshield
softball	sweatshirt	toothpick	watercolor	wishbone
spacecraft	sweetheart	touchdown	waterfall	woodpecker
splashdown	teacup	turtleneck	waterfront	woodwork
spotlight	teenage	undercover	watermelon	wristband
springboard	textbook	underground	weatherman	wristwatch
stairway	thumbtack	uptown	weekend	

RHYMING WORDS

can—ran
sat—hat
bell—sell
bed—fed
sent—went
bone—stone
fight—light
late—state
think—stink
sun—fun
thin—spin
game—name
send—bend
beat—seat
cow—plow
thank—drank
ship—skip
lake—shake
bring—thing

clock—lock
cat—fat
call—mall
bag—tag
hide—ride
bark—dark
bank—thank
nut—hut
nose—rose
another—mother
shoulder—boulder
does—dozen
easel—weasel
eagle—beagle
drift—sift
dream—cream
double—trouble
creek—peak
court—port

could—would
couch—pouch
kettle—metal
jewels—tools
polite—delight
height—fright
healthy—wealthy
ground—sound
needy—greedy
glisten—listen
fierce—pierce
enter—center
owl—howl
outline—define
pony—phony
plastic—elastic
pickles—nickels
stream—steam

WORD FAMILIES

b<u>at</u>	b<u>ay</u>	b<u>ake</u>	b<u>ill</u>
br<u>at</u>	clay	br<u>ake</u>	d<u>ill</u>
c<u>at</u>	d<u>ay</u>	c<u>ake</u>	f<u>ill</u>
ch<u>at</u>	g<u>ay</u>	f<u>ake</u>	h<u>ill</u>
f<u>at</u>	gr<u>ay</u>	l<u>ake</u>	J<u>ill</u>
fl<u>at</u>	h<u>ay</u>	m<u>ake</u>	k<u>ill</u>
gn<u>at</u>	l<u>ay</u>	qu<u>ake</u>	m<u>ill</u>
h<u>at</u>	m<u>ay</u>	r<u>ake</u>	qu<u>ill</u>
m<u>at</u>	p<u>ay</u>	s<u>ake</u>	p<u>ill</u>
r<u>at</u>	play	sh<u>ake</u>	sk<u>ill</u>
s<u>at</u>	pr<u>ay</u>	sl<u>ake</u>	sp<u>ill</u>
sp<u>at</u>	r<u>ay</u>	sn<u>ake</u>	st<u>ill</u>
th<u>at</u>	s<u>ay</u>	st<u>ake</u>	w<u>ill</u>
	st<u>ay</u>	t<u>ake</u>	
	tr<u>ay</u>	w<u>ake</u>	

____an	____ing	____ank
____ip	____in	____eer
____out	____it	____un
____ink	____one	____ave
____eak	____ed	____en
____ame	____ent	____ope
____eat	____ap	____ee
____ed	____od	____ick
____ot	____ock	____ight
____all	____ack	____ip
____ell	____end	____ow
____ear	____ag	____ail
____uff	____ain	____ab
____ate	____ump	____ump
____ide	____ap	____ite

301

CONTEXT CLUE SENTENCES

1. The child looked sad and _____.
2. The puppy ran _____ the street.
3. The turtle _____ its mouth.
4. The glass was _____.
5. It is time to go to _____.
6. School is very _____.
7. We _____ the game.
8. It was time to _____.
9. The _____ was on.
10. It is later than I _____.
11. We wrapped the _____.
12. Father sat in a _____ chair.
13. The horse _____ at me.
14. The ghost _____.
15. It is time to clean up your _____.
16. I caught a _____.
17. My pen ran out of _____.
18. An alligator has sharp _____.
19. This book was _____.
20. The best part of the day is _____.
21. I rode on the _____.
22. The bus was _____.
23. The eagle flew across the _____.
24. A lazy old _____ slept in the sun.
25. We _____ the noise.
26. The _____ came out of the cave.
27. The _____ flew away on her broom.
28. The car was in the _____.
29. The man was cold and _____.
30. The boat _____ on the water.